FACT-FINDERS

Special Investigations to Develop Research Skills

Grades 4–8

by Barbara Simpson

DALE SEYMOUR PUBLICATIONS

The author wishes to acknowledge the following people for their love, support, and encouragement:
Mark Johnsen-Harris and my colleagues at The Wheeler School
Catherine Valentino
Lynn Latson
Beverly Cory
my parents
my husband John and son Matthew, who mean the world to me

This book is dedicated to the children of The Wheeler School in Providence, Rhode Island.

Cover design: Lucy McCargar
Calligraphy: Barbara Simpson
Illustrations: Mitchell Rose

Order number DS13701
ISBN 0-86651-349-3

abcdefghi-MA-893210987

Contents

Introduction

Fact-Finders contains 30 challenging research projects appropriate for students in grades 4 through 8. The research involved covers a wide variety of subjects, many of which will be new to your students. The projects build on young people's natural curiosity about the world and on their fascination with odd facts. The main purpose of the projects is, of course, not to teach students the odd facts, but to teach them *how to find* those facts; to whet their appetites for research and expose them to new sources of information—wonderful fact books, such as almanacs and the provocative *Book of Lists* volumes, that many budding researchers find intrinsically motivating.

Often, what "research" means to students in the middle grades is going off with a particular topic to hit the encyclopedia and write a report based on their findings. You've probably seen that even when students enthusiastically dive into their research, that enthusiasm wanes when they realize that they don't know quite where to begin; don't know what they should take notes on because there's so much information; and, likely as not, end up writing a report that is in large measure copied straight from the encyclopedia.

This book offers an alternative to that approach to research. The *Fact-Finders* projects focus on the *process* of doing research rather than on the writing of a formal research report. These projects allow students to concentrate their energies and imaginations on solving puzzles and locating specific facts, while getting to know and use their library's card catalog and reference shelves, without having to tackle the broader tasks of organization and writing.

This doesn't mean, of course, that these investigations have to be limited to basic fact-finding. Many of the projects suggest creative or imaginative extensions to be done after the initial fact-finding has been completed, plus bonus activities for the most intrigued students who would enjoy pursuing the research even further. Based on several years of experience with this approach, I find that middle-school students who get excited about the process of research through "fact-finding" are more relaxed and thus more likely to succeed when assigned the traditional research-and-report-writing projects at a later time.

Locating and Listing Resources

This book will take your students beyond the four walls of your classroom into school and public libraries, even perhaps to local colleges, to museums, to the community newspaper, to businesses, to special organizations—wherever they think they might find the facts they need. The sources of information I used in creating the *Fact-*

Finders projects are indicated in the Answer Guide (page 93) and listed in the Research Resources (page 104). You may want to do some groundwork to see which of these sources are available to your students in your school library or public libraries, and perhaps ask that they be kept on reserve so that one student doesn't check them out and prevent others from using them.

It is often helpful to give younger students hints about what sources to use, whereas older students generally enjoy the challenge of discovering sources by themselves. In so doing, they often come across alternative sources as good as or better than mine. There is certainly no need to restrict the students to the references listed in this book, as long as they document the sources they use.

Bibliographic form. For the purpose of these projects, it is of vital importance that the students keep track of their sources during their investigations. Being able to document sources is a key ingredient to any type of research. On page 107 I have included a sheet that shows the bibliographic forms for different sources that students are likely to use. You can duplicate this sheet as a handout and distribute it to students to keep for reference as they collect their research. Note that styles for bibliographic form vary somewhat; if you have taught students other forms, by all means have them follow those. Recording the information is more important than the style in which it is recorded. It should be a requirement that students turn in a list of their sources with the answers for any project.

The Answer Guide. An Answer Guide has been provided at the end of this book for your convenience and information. I call it a "guide" rather than a "key" because I don't want these regarded as the definitive answers. You and your students will likely find, as I did, that information is reported differently in different sources and that some "facts" may be disputed; additionally, many facts will change with the passage of time. Please remain flexible and open-minded in accepting answers that vary from those reported here, as long as your students have carefully documented their sources and can prove the existence of other reasonable answers.

Using the Projects

The *Fact-Finders* projects are extremely flexible and can be adapted to any of several uses in your classroom.

- You might assign particular projects to be completed for a grade.
- You might allow students to freely choose among the projects for extra credit.
- Individual students can strike out on their own, tackling the projects that most interest them.
- A group of students interested in the same topic can seek facts together, completing the project as a cooperative effort.
- You might assign the whole class a particular project, with each student responsible for part of the research.
- You might let each student select a project as homework, allowing them to work with parents or other family members in finding the information.

Depending on your approach, the time spent on each project can be open-ended, or it might be limited to a specific interval, such as one week, one month, or one marking period.

Making "research boxes." I originally modeled these projects after the Challenge Boxes program developed by Catherine Valentino. (For a description of her program, see the *Challenge Boxes* book, published by Dale Seymour Publications, 1983). Thus I have always presented these *Fact-Finders* activities to my students as independent study projects. I store each project in a box large enough to hold reference books, notebooks, and papers. On the outside of the box, I place a colorful, motivating "advertisement" (based on the lead-in sentence that begins each *Fact-Finders* project) to entice students to try that project. Inside the box, they find the instruction card and any task cards or specialty cards appropriate to individual projects. Since each box is reused many times by different students, the pieces inside must be durable. You might duplicate the various elements on heavier stock, or laminate them to sheets of tagboard. Adding color to the cards yourself (or enlisting the aid of artistically inclined students) contributes greatly to the projects' appeal.

Of course, it is not necessary to set up an elaborate library of "research boxes." Instead, you can simply duplicate the parts of single projects and distribute them to individual students, to small groups, or to the whole class, as you prefer.

A pocket folder is a convenient organizing device; as students collect information, the folder gives them one place to keep it together. You might ask that the entire folder be handed in when the activity has been completed, with bibliographies in one pocket, answers and creative extensions in the other. An optional answer sheet on which students can record their research findings is included on page 106 of this book.

Holding conferences. After students have had a chance to work on one or more projects, it's always valuable to plan a conference, preferably with an individual child or with small groups, to talk about the research process and ask students to explain how they attacked their different tasks. During these conversations you will discover the learning experiences that the children encountered and see how they overcame problems along the way. If you do this in small groups, students can learn new approaches from one another. Such conferences sometimes point out areas where a particular unit of study might be helpful—for example, how to use an index or a table of contents to locate information in a book.

Final awards. You can recognize students' work on these projects in a variety of ways. You might simply grant academic or report card credit for successfully completed projects, or you could establish a goal—such as completing 10 projects—and present special award certificates to students who reach that goal. A reproducible certificate for this purpose is provided on page 108 of this book. In some instances you might want to display final projects in your classroom or in the school library, or have the students share their findings in an assembly or as part of a presentation to another classroom.

Some Parting Thoughts

It feels highly appropriate that I sit here in my public library writing this introduction to you, after all the hours I've spent in libraries researching the *Fact-Finders* projects. It all started a few years ago when I, a fourth-grade teacher at The Wheeler School, first met Catherine Valentino and learned about the creative independent study projects she calls Challenge Boxes. Inspired by her example and encouraged by my principal, I spent an entire summer vacation devising independent study projects of my own for students in our school to use the following fall.

I had a field day developing these projects. The library became my home away from home, and my fact-finding explorations through its bookshelves introduced me to many intriguing people, places, and events, and to the often-curious facts that mark mankind's winding path through history. I couldn't get enough of the fascinating information I was uncovering! Some of the projects in this book date back to that first summer; others have been designed in subsequent summers or when an idea grabbed me and wouldn't let go.

It is my sincere hope that through the *Fact-Finders* investigations, your students will become as excited as I did about the treasures to be discovered through research, and that they will eagerly share with you and with each other the wonders they find.

Barbara Simpson

PROJECT 1 Travel the world, but watch out for those out-of-date road signs, maps, and globes!

New (Old) Names for Old (New) Places

HE EARTH keeps spinning round and round, but historical events have changed the names of cities and countries through the years. For example, did you know that New York was called New Netherlands in the 1600s, and that New York City was called New Amsterdam? Changes like that are still happening. As recently as 1980, the name of the country of Rhodesia in Africa was changed to Zimbabwe.

You have two tasks to complete in this globe-trotting activity:

- Discover the former names of the 16 places that are listed on Activity Card 1.
- Uncover the modern names of the 16 places once known by the obsolete names listed on Activity Card 2.

NEW (OLD) NAMES FOR OLD (NEW) PLACES — ACTIVITY CARD 1

What were these places called in days gone by? List the resources where you find your information.

1. Chicago
2. Ethiopia
3. Ghana
4. Hawaii
5. Indonesia
6. Istanbul
7. Leningrad
8. Malawi
9. Namibia
10. Ontario
11. Oslo
12. Suriname
13. Tanzania
14. Tokyo
15. Zambia
16. Zaire

BONUS: Find out if the town or city where you live was ever called by another name.

NEW (OLD) NAMES FOR OLD (NEW) PLACES — ACTIVITY CARD 2

What are the up-to-date names of these places? List the resources where you find your information.

1. Batavia
2. British Honduras
3. Ceylon
4. Ciudad Trujillo
5. Danzig
6. East Pakistan
7. Formosa
8. Fort Duquense
9. Fort Rouille
10. Hesperia
11. Illyria
12. Persia
13. Saigon
14. Siam
15. Stalingrad
16. Tenochtitlán

PROJECT 2 You're an undercover agent on the trail of some mysterious folks!

SHORT STUFF

HEN PEOPLE become famous, sometimes they prefer not to use the full names they were given at birth. Some people use just their initials instead of their first and middle names. Others become better known by a nickname. In either case, their "real" identity is a mystery to the rest of us.

This challenging activity dares you to become an undercover agent and expose the secret identities of the people listed on the activity cards. You have two tasks for each card:

- Discover the full name of each person listed.
- Tell why each person is famous.

SHORT STUFF

ACTIVITY CARD 1

What are their full names and why are they famous? List the resources where you find your information.

1. A. A. Milne
2. B. F. Goodrich
3. J. C. Penney
4. H. G. Wells
5. W. C. Fields
6. J. R. R. Tolkien
7. P. K. Wrigley
8. e. e. cummings
9. P. T. Barnum
10. T. S. Eliot

SHORT STUFF

ACTIVITY CARD 2

What are their real names and why are they famous? List the resources where you find your information.

1. "Johnny Appleseed"
2. "Jelly Roll" Morton
3. "Grandma Moses"
4. "Dr. Seuss"
5. "OJ" Simpson
6. "Molly Pitcher"
7. "Groucho" Marx
8. "Annie Oakley"
9. "Babe" Ruth
10. "Ladybird" Johnson

PROJECT 3 Upon close inspection, some things are just *not* what they seem. Confront this activity and prove that nobody can fool you!

Secret Identities

IS IT OR ISN'T it what it appears? You may find it hard to believe, but the items listed on the activity card are NOT all what they seem to be. Which ones are hiding their true identities behind a confusing name? Educate yourself and others as you discover their true identities.

SECRET IDENTITIES ACTIVITY CARD

Discover the true identity of each item below. List the resources where you find your information.

1. Is a peanut really a nut?
2. Is a woolly bear really a bear?
3. Is a horned toad really a toad?
4. Is shoofly pie really pie?
5. Is dry cleaning really dry?
6. Is an electric eel really electric?
7. Is a shooting star really a star?
8. Is a geoduck really a duck?
9. Is a guinea pig really a pig?
10. Is a cowbird really a bird?
11. Is a banana tree really a tree?
12. Are coffee beans really beans?
13. Is a breadfruit really a fruit?
14. Is shortbread really bread?
15. Is an English horn really English and really a horn?
16. Is a lead pencil really made with lead?
17. Are there really beans in a bean bag?
18. Is your funny bone really a bone?
19. Is a firefly really a fly?
20. Is a wood duck really a duck?
21. Is a silkworm really a worm?
22. Is rice paper really made from rice?
23. Is a prairie dog really a dog?
24. Is foam rubber really rubber?
25. Is a starfish really a fish?
26. Is a silverfish really a fish?
27. Is a bald eagle really bald?
28. Are black-eyed peas really peas?

PROJECT 4 Why don't people ever say what they mean? Find the "truth" behind these common sayings.

YOU DON'T SAY!

T'S VERY LIKELY that you have heard or used the common expressions listed on the activity card. However, have you ever thought about what those expressions actually mean? Perhaps the real question is, what do we mean by *meaning*? All these phrases have figurative meanings, but we could also read them literally. This activity asks you to explore them from both angles.

Choose at least six of the expressions on the activity card. Do some research to find out what they would mean if we took them *literally*. (If you can't find an exact measurement, give your best estimate based on the information you have found.) Then, in your own words, explain the *figurative* meaning of each one.

YOU DON'T SAY! ACTIVITY CARD

Write the literal and figurative meanings for at least six of these expressions. Be sure to keep track of the resources you use.

1. I knew him when he was knee-high to a grasshopper!
   (Literally, how tall?)
2. I like her, but she has a really thin skin!
   (Literally, how thin?)
3. My uncle eats like a horse!
   (Literally, how much is that?)
4. Quick as a wink, she was gone.
   (Literally, how fast is that?)
5. He followed us at a snail's pace all the way home.
   (Literally, how fast is that?)
6. I'm up to my neck in homework!
   (Literally, how deep is that?)
7. In arguing with the principal, she's skating on thin ice.
   (Literally, how thin is that?)
8. Why, your book bag is light as a feather!
   (Literally, how light is that?)
9. The news hit me like a ton of bricks.
   (Literally, how many bricks is that?)
10. A picture is worth a thousand words.
    (Literally, how much are 1000 words worth?)
11. The new rapid transit is faster than a speeding bullet.
    (Literally, how fast is that?)
12. Their opinion isn't worth a hill of beans.
    (Literally, how much is a hill of beans worth?)

PROJECT 5 It's not Noah's Ark or the National Zoo, but animal-lovers can hop, slither, and leap right into this activity!

MENAGERIE MEDLEY

OU HAVE JUST been chosen as an assistant to the renowned zoologist Dr. Bentley, who collects animals for zoos around the world. Dr. Bentley knows the scientific classifications for all the animals but is less familiar with the obscure terms that people sometimes use for animal groups, such as "a muster of peacocks" or "an exaltation of larks." The good doctor is also easily confused by the various names for animal young, and has been heard to mutter, "Pups, kits, cubs, what's the difference!"

One of your jobs as Dr. Bentley's assistant is to research the special terms for animal groups and for different animal babies. (You'll find that not all sources agree. Be sure to write down the references you use.)

Choose one or more of the four activity cards. When you have completed the assignment, make a picture dictionary for Dr. Bentley, demonstrating the results of your research.

MENAGERIE MEDLEY ACTIVITY CARD 1

Find the collective names that are sometimes applied to these animal groups.

1. a group of partridges
2. a group of badgers
3. a group of lions
4. a group of wolves
5. a group of hawks
6. a group of geese
7. a group of leopards
8. a group of foxes
9. a group of bears
10. a group of rhinoceroses

BONUS: How many more group names can you find?

MENAGERIE MEDLEY ACTIVITY CARD 2

Some group names are commonly used for several types of animals. List all the animals you can find whose collective group is called . . .

1. a herd
2. a flock
3. a colony
4. a troop
5. a pod

What similarities can you find among animals who share the same group name?

MENAGERIE MEDLEY ACTIVITY CARD 3

What is the name for each of these animal babies?

1. a baby oyster
2. a baby swan
3. a baby turkey
4. a baby pig
5. a baby kangaroo
6. a baby goose
7. a baby zebra
8. a baby eel
9. a baby hawk
10. a baby salmon
11. a baby quail
12. a baby pigeon

BONUS: How many more special names for animal young can you find?

MENAGERIE MEDLEY ACTIVITY CARD 4

Some animal babies are called by the same name. List all the animals you can find whose babies are called . . .

1. cubs
2. kits or kittens
3. pups
4. calves

What similarities can you find among the baby animals who share the same name?

PROJECT 6 Felix Unger and Oscar Madison were known as "the odd couple," but wait till you see *these* unusual pairs!

MIXED-UP MATCHES

TWO OF A KIND? Walt Disney was the father of Mickey Mouse, and Ernest Hemingway was a big-game hunter and prize-winning author. Those two may not seem to have much in common, but if you dig into their lives, you'll find that both men drove ambulances in World War I. That makes them a matching pair!

Take a look at each unusual pair listed on the activity card. Then complete these two tasks:

- Using the questions as clues, do some research to find out what the folks in each pair have in common.
- Choose one pair and write a dialogue between the two in which they discuss their common interest and do a little bragging about their own accomplishments.

Be sure to cite your sources of information.

1. **Louisa May Alcott and Laura Ingalls Wilder**
   Alcott and Wilder fall at opposite ends of the alphabet, yet we might find these two authors close to each other in a library card catalog. Why?
2. **Jim Davis and Don Marquis**
   Both became well known for their work in newspapers, but at different times and in different sections of the paper. What common elements would you find in their work?
3. **George Washington and Sir John Alexander MacDonald**
   They lived in different centuries, but they might have brought home similar stories from "the office." Why?
4. **Mark Twain and Agatha Christie**
   Twain's specialty was humor, Christie's was mystery, yet these two writers have something in common. What might that be?
5. **Mother Teresa and Linus Pauling**
   Mother Teresa is the world's most famous nun, while Pauling made his name as a chemist. Why might you find these two names on the same list?
6. **Sally Ride and Valentina Tereshkova**
   One grew up in the United States, the other in the Soviet Union. But if they met at a party, they would have something in common to talk about. What is it?
7. **Mary Shelley and Boris Karloff**
   Shelley was a 19th-century writer married to a famous romantic poet. Karloff is a movie actor who specializes in horror films. What can these two possibly have in common?
8. **Bing Crosby and Bill Haley**
   Crosby was a mellow-voiced crooner of the 30's and 40's, while Haley and his group were among the earliest rock-and-roll stars in the 50's. They likely did not have the same fans, but they do have one thing in common. What can it be?
9. **Mel Blanc and Tokyo Rose**
   These two shared a mode of expression—but for very different purposes. For what "feature" were both well known?
10. **Junko Tabei and Sir Edmund Hillary**
    This Japanese woman and New Zealand man both reached the top in their field. What feat do they have in common?

PROJECT 7 Hop aboard the Zany Express to compete in the International Cow Chip Throwing Contest and 39 other crackbrained championships!

CRAZY CONTESTS

O YOU LOVE contests? Then step right up and take this one-of-a-kind tour of the United States. Our travel agent has organized an extraordinary excursion for contest-lovers everywhere. Your destination: the sites of the wackiest contests ever imagined.

There are 40 different contests listed on the activity card. You have two tasks:

- Discover the location of 20 of these contests. (Some of them may be held in more than one place.)
- Draw or obtain an outline map of the United States. Mark the location of the contests you have found, using a daffy symbol that makes clear which contest is held there.

BONUS: For each contest you locate, explain in one or two sentences why it is appropriate for that particular contest to be held in that particular place.

CRAZY CONTESTS

ACTIVITY CARD

1. World Championship Duck Calling Contest **2.** Hot Dog Eating Contest **3.** World Championship Pillowfighting Contest **4.** Great Crab Crawl **5.** National Rotten Sneaker Contest **6.** Riding Lawnmower Race **7.** Grape Stomping Contest

8. Beard Contest **9.** Speed Jumprope Contest **10.** Miss Drumstick Contest **11.** Goat Races **12.** World Smelt Eating Contest **13.** Hoop Rolling Contest **14.** Great Bed Race **15.** World Championship Sled Dog Races **16.** Milk Carton Boat Race Classic **17.** International Brick and Rolling Pin Throwing Contest **18.** Hollerin' Contest **19.** Tom Sawyer Fence Painting Contest **20.** World Championship Slingshot Tournament **21.** Camel Races World Championship **22.** International Worm Fiddling Contest **23.** World Championship Watermelon Seed Spitting Contest

24. Pet Rock Race **25.** Snowshoe Softball Tournament **26.** World's Largest Egg Contest **27.** Lobster Land Race **28.** World Championship Inner Tube Race **29.** Bed-Making Championship **30.** International Cow Chip Throwing Contest **31.** Waiter's Race **32.** International Stone Skipping Tournament **33.** Mule Pulling Contest **34.** Frog Eating Contest **35.** Yo-yo Olympics **36.** World Hot Air Balloon Championship **37.** National Marbles Olympics **38.** Rooster Crowing Contest **39.** Jumping Frog Jubilee **40.** International Pancake Day Race

PROJECT 8 Brain teasers to tickle your fancy and make you wonder . . .

TRIVIA TRICKSTERS I

HOUSANDS OF FACTS about the world are things we take for granted, things we never question, or things we just never take the time to learn. Much of this information can be called TRIVIA because it's obscure or because it seems unimportant compared with other "worthwhile" things we feel we should know.

The catch is that trivia is fun and intriguing. What's more, people who are trivia buffs can use what they know to tickle and tease everyone else. And that's fun, too.

If you feel like mastering some trivia, choose at least eight of the trivia tricksters on the activity card and research them. Write up your answers and tell where you found your information.

TRIVIA TRICKSTERS I — ACTIVITY CARD

1. Why is it almost impossible to drown in the Dead Sea?
2. "Jackdaws love my big sphinx of quartz." Apart from the fact that it sounds like nonsense, what is so unusual about this sentence?
3. Why is a calf sometimes made to swallow a magnet right after it is born?
4. Why are flamingos not naturally pink?
5. What are three sporting events that are won by people moving backwards?
6. How could Gladys Gooding have played for the New York Rangers, the New York Knicks, and the Brooklyn Dodgers in a single year?
7. What is the order of flavors in a Life Savers "five flavors" candy roll? Is it always the same?
8. What was the first word said on the moon? What was the first sentence?
9. Is it possible for someone working in a skyscraper to get motion sickness on windy days? Why or why not?
10. How can plants grow in the Atacama Desert in Chile when no rainfall has ever been recorded there?

PROJECT 9 Just in case you're hooked, here's more trivia to pursue!

TRIVIA TRICKSTERS II

HE TRIVIA CATEGORIES this time are Space, Geography, Physiology, Sports, Nature, and General Knowledge. Do you consider yourself a master of any of those areas? Show what you can do! Your challenge is to choose at least eight of the trivia tricksters on the activity card and research them. Prepare your answers as a written report and tell where you found your information.

1. Can any man-made structure on earth be seen from the moon? What evidence of civilization have astronauts seen with the unaided eye while orbiting earth?
2. Quito, the capital of Ecuador, sits almost on the equator in "the torrid zone." Yet Quito's climate is said to be one of perpetual spring. How can this be?
3. How can someone catch a fish in the Sahara Desert when there is no river or lake in sight?
4. Why do humans shiver when they are cold?
5. The Houston Astros once had a home game rained out, but they play indoors. How can that be?
6. Why were barns and old-fashioned schoolhouses traditionally painted red?
7. Every year, the earth gains weight. How?
8. Explain how it is possible to look into space to see the beginning of the universe.
9. Why do ducks never get wet?
10. What makes the porcupine an excellent swimmer?

PROJECT 10 Know anyone whose favorite book is the dictionary? Etymologists of the world, unite!

SUPER SLEUTH I

ID YOU KNOW that every word you use has a hidden story behind it? If you track down those stories, you can learn a lot about times long ago and the people who lived then. Some of the stories are more interesting than others. Many are strange and full of surprises.

This activity gives you 24 wonderful words. Your task is to select at least 12 of those words and discover the history behind them. Be sure to note the sources from which you get your information. (Hint: To research word origins, you might start by looking in your library card catalog under "English Language—Etymology.")

BONUS: Choose 5 additional words of your own that you would like to research.

1. spaghetti	2. clue	3. clodhopper
4. diaper	5. bride	6. slapstick
7. coward	8. denim	9. elbow
10. kangaroo	11. CORDUROY	12. lollipop

13. carousel	14. pretzel	15. hippopotamus
16. doodle	17. portholes	18. canter
19. marathon	20. carat	21. genuine
22. chow	23. mummy	24. QUIZ

PROJECT 11 WANTED: One good detective. There are plenty of cases to be solved . . . but only word-lovers need apply.

SUPER SLEUTH II

ONE SOURCE OF information about word derivation is the dictionary, but sometimes that tells only part of the story. There are other books that do nothing but explore the strange and fascinating histories of the words we use every day. If you did Super Sleuth I, you may have already found some of these books.

Now here are 24 more words to challenge your research skills. Choose 15 of these words and see what you can discover about their origins. Be sure to write down the sources of your information.

BONUS: A Super Sleuth II Award goes to anyone who can track down the stories behind all 24 words!

1. sabotage	2. purple	3. pumpernickel
4. khaki	5. scuba	6. pipsqueak
7. UMBRELLA	8. tulip	9. thinking cap
10. dandelion	11. KETCHUP	12. mustache

13. muscles	14. cereal	15. eggs Benedict
16. polka dots	17. perfume	18. racket
19. bleachers	20. salary	21. marshmallow
22. panic	23. barber	24. coconut

PROJECT 12 Six, five, four, three, two, one . . .
Counting was never so much fun!

NUTTY NUMBERS

URE YOU can count to 10. That's easy. Bet you could find the answer to 54 times 87, or even 623,896 divided by 7 if you HAD to! But beyond that, how's your number sense? Do you know how deep is the deep blue sea? Or how many words are defined in an unabridged dictionary? Or what is the top speed of a race horse? And if you don't know, do you know where to look to find out?

Here's a chance to see how good you are with numbers. Choose one of the activity cards and complete these three steps:

- First, write down your best guess for each number.
- Second, research to find out the real answer. Be sure to note the sources of your information.
- Finally, compute the difference between your guess and the actual number.

Set up a chart to record all this information.

NUTTY NUMBERS — ACTIVITY CARD 1

Write your guess; then find out the actual . . .

1. Number of dimples on a golf ball.
2. Number of ones on a paper dollar, excluding serial numbers.
3. Number of consecutive baseball games played by Lou Gehrig.
4. Number of intersecting lines on a go board.
5. Number of players on a polo team.
6. Number of signers of the Declaration of Independence.
7. Number of known moons orbiting Jupiter.
8. Amount of money each player is given at the start of a Monopoly game.
9. Number of stitches on a regulation baseball.
10. Air distance from London to Cape Town.
11. Distance between the stakes in a game of horseshoes.
12. Length of time Robinson Crusoe spent on his island.

NUTTY NUMBERS — ACTIVITY CARD 2

Write your guess; then find out the actual . . .

1. Height of Mount Everest.
2. Number of carats in the Hope Diamond.
3. Number of strings on a harp.
4. Length of the Nile River.
5. Total amount if you double one cent every day for 30 days.
6. Number of faces on a truncated icosahedron.
7. Number of spokes on a typical 26-inch bicycle wheel.
8. Length of the Verrazano-Narrows Bridge.
9. Distance from the ground to the top of a regulation volleyball net.
10. Average life expectancy of the ostrich.
11. Noise level in the average factory (in decibels).
12. Average number of hairs growing on the human head.

PROJECT 13 How would you like to make your living as a "kiss mixer"? If you're interested, apply here!

Odd Jobs

HEN YOU GROW UP, you could be a doctor, an astronaut, a professional baseball player, a movie director, a computer programmer, or a lion tamer. The list of things you could do is endless! For every job you can think of, there are probably 100 more that you never even dreamed existed. Before you make up your mind, you might consider one of the unusual-sounding jobs on the activity cards.

Choose one of the activity cards and complete these two tasks:

- Give descriptions of at least 10 of the occupations listed.
- For each occupation that you identify, find the name and location of a company or organization that might be willing to hire somone in that job.

If, after all your "labors," you still can't decide on a career, don't worry. You can be almost anything you try to be . . . and you can always change your mind!

ODD JOBS

ACTIVITY CARD 1

Have you considered a career as one of these?

1. BELLY BUILDER
2. DUKEY RIDER
3. FOOT STRAIGHTENER
4. KISS MIXER
5. LEGEND MAKER
6. BEST BOY
7. BUTTON LAYER
8. LAST CHALKER
9. ANTISQUEAK FILLER
10. MAGAZINE REPAIRER
11. PAD HAND
12. BUNDLER
13. ROOTER OPERATOR
14. HAY SORTER
15. PONY EDGER
16. MOTHER REPAIRER

ODD JOBS

ACTIVITY CARD 2

If you were one of these, how would you spend your days?

1. GRAPHOLOGIST
2. SIFFLEUR
3. CRYPTANALYST
4. CALLIGRAPHER
5. MYCOLOGIST
6. LIBRETTIST
7. MOSAICIST
8. CHEF DE FROID
9. STEVEDORE
10. GLAZIER
11. ROUSTABOUT
12. DRAFTER
13. ARCHIVIST
14. COUTURIER
15. FUNAMBULIST
16. OTORHINOLARYNGOLOGIST

PROJECT 14 News flash! Special alert! Strange new words invade English language! Details at 11 . . . or on instruction card!

HOT OFF THE PRESS

EVERY YEAR, a few new words and phrases manage to sneak their way into the dictionary. No, they're not secret agents sent from Roget's thesaurus, trying to wreak havoc with the alphabetization. They are legitimate words and phrases representing new inventions, fads, and other modern phenomena.

All such words are genuine additions to the English language. For example, the term "freeze-dried" was never used before 1949, when the process was first developed, and it didn't come into common use until the 1960s. But now it's likely here to stay.

The challenge of this activity is two fold:

- List at least 20 words or phrases that have materialized within the past 50 years.
- Next to each word you list, document the decade or approximate year of its appearance, or give a reason why it could not have been around longer than 50 years.

PROJECT 15 Make sure you "collect" yourself before getting into this activity!

Collector's Edition

ACK RATS, unite! A popular pasttime among people of all ages is collecting a particular type of object—baseball cards, T-shirts, restaurant menus, hats, pennants, bottle caps, match books, key chains, bumper stickers . . . . You name it, and most probably someone in the world spends time collecting it.

You have two activity cards to choose from in this activity.

1. The first card lists the special names for hobbies that involve collections, and you must discover what items are being collected.
2. The second card tells what is being collected, and your task is to discover the special name for the collector.

BONUS: Whichever card you choose, find and list the names of people who collect each of the items indicated on the card. Be sure to give the sources of your information!

COLLECTOR'S EDITION

ACTIVITY CARD 1

What are you likely to find around the house of someone who is interested in . . .

1. cagophily
2. deltiology
3. errinophily
4. laclabphily
5. numismatics
6. philately
7. phillumney
8. philometry
9. receptary

COLLECTOR'S EDITION | ACTIVITY CARD 2

What would you call . . .

1. a collector of teddy bears
2. a collector of subway tokens
3. a collector of birds' eggs
4. a collector of autographs
5. a collector of dolls
6. a collector of shells
7. a collector of butterflies
8. a collector of inn signs
9. a collector of phonograph records

PROJECT 16 Mmm-mm! What smells so good? Become a "galloping gourmet" and take a whiff of this!

WHAT'S COOKING?

YOU MAY HAVE eaten many different gastronomic delicacies in your lifetime, but do you know the ingredients that were used in their preparation? This activity is a test for your deductive powers as well as your taste buds. And it's not hard to figure out where you'll need to research to confirm your answers!

We have borrowed some recipe cards from the files of the Secret Chef. You have two tasks in this activity:

- Choose 15 of the recipe cards from the Secret Chef's kitchen and name the dish that can be prepared with each. Give a source that confirms your answer.
- Choose 2 of the recipes and double them; choose 2 more recipes and cut them in half. Write out the results and tell how many servings you would get with each.

Fair warning: For any recipe, there are many possible slight variations, both in the ingredients and in the amounts. Don't feel that you have to find a recipe that exactly matches the Secret Chef's recipe. Just be sure it's the same basic dish.

$1\frac{1}{2}$ lb. chestnuts
water
1 cup butter
$1\frac{1}{2}$ cups diced celery
1 cup chopped onions
1 tsp. thyme
1 tsp. marjoram
$\frac{1}{2}$ tsp. pepper
8 cups fresh bread crumbs
2 tsp. salt
• *MAKES 11 CUPS* •

RECIPE CARD 1

1 lb. ground beef
1 large onion, chopped
1 green pepper, chopped
$3\frac{1}{2}$ cups canned tomatoes
1 (1-lb.) can kidney beans
1 bay leaf
2 T. chili powder
2 tsp. salt
$\frac{1}{8}$ tsp. cayenne pepper
$\frac{1}{8}$ tsp. paprika
• *MAKES 6 SERVINGS* •

RECIPE CARD 2

$\frac{2}{3}$ cup mayonnaise
1 tsp. salt
4 to 5 cups cut-up, cooked chicken
2 tsp. grated onion
2 T. cider vinegar
1 cup sliced celery
1 cup minced green pepper
romaine or iceberg lettuce leaves
• *MAKES 6 to 8 SERVINGS* •

RECIPE CARD 3

4 cups dry navy beans
4 tsp. salt
$\frac{3}{4}$ cup dark molasses
$\frac{1}{2}$ cup packed dark brown sugar
1 T. dry mustard
1 tsp. pepper
1 large onion, studded with 4 cloves
$\frac{1}{2}$ lb. salt pork, with rind slashed
• *MAKES 12 SERVINGS* •

RECIPE CARD 4

3 cups tomato juice
3 T. olive or salad oil
3 large tomatoes, peeled and seeded
1 cucumber, peeled and seeded
1 small onion, chopped
1 small green pepper, chopped
1 garlic clove
1 tsp. sugar
3/4 tsp. salt
1/2 tsp. hot pepper sauce
•MAKES 4 SERVINGS•

RECIPE CARD 5

Hollandaise sauce
4 eggs
2 English muffins
butter or margarine
4 slices Canadian bacon or ham
•MAKES 4 SERVINGS•

RECIPE CARD 6

pastry for 1 pie crust
1 T. butter, softened
12 bacon slices
4 eggs
2 cups heavy cream
3/4 tsp salt
1/8 tsp. nutmeg
1/4 lb. Swiss cheese , shredded (1 cup)
• MAKES 6 SERVINGS •

RECIPE CARD 7

2 lb. lean ground beef
2 cups fresh bread crumbs (about 4 slices)
2 tsp. salt
1/2 cup milk
1/2 cup minced onion
2 eggs
1/4 tsp. pepper
2 T. catsup
1 T. Worcestershire sauce
• MAKES 8 SERVINGS •

RECIPE CARD 8

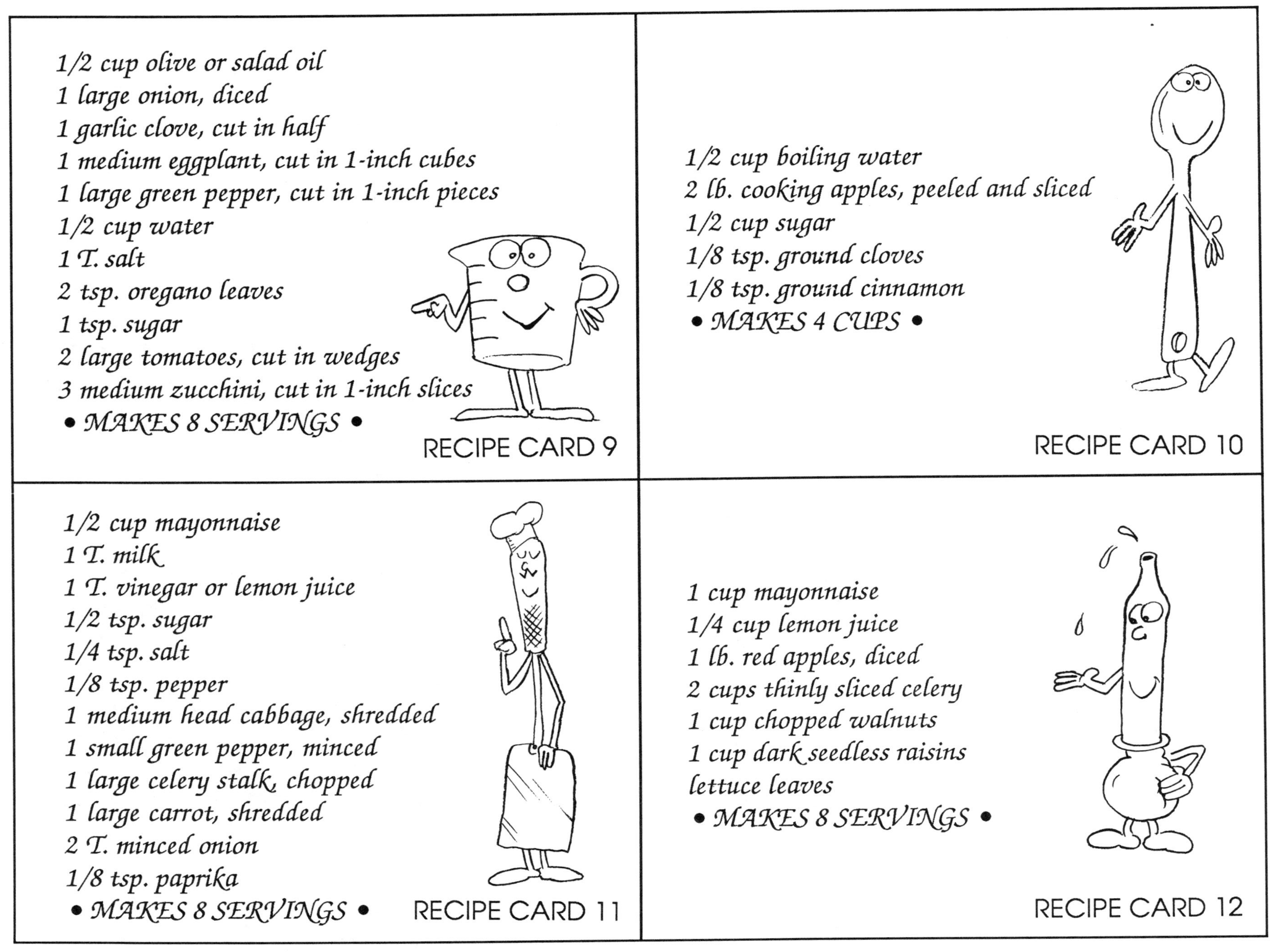

1/2 cup olive or salad oil
1 large onion, diced
1 garlic clove, cut in half
1 medium eggplant, cut in 1-inch cubes
1 large green pepper, cut in 1-inch pieces
1/2 cup water
1 T. salt
2 tsp. oregano leaves
1 tsp. sugar
2 large tomatoes, cut in wedges
3 medium zucchini, cut in 1-inch slices
• MAKES 8 SERVINGS •

RECIPE CARD 9

1/2 cup boiling water
2 lb. cooking apples, peeled and sliced
1/2 cup sugar
1/8 tsp. ground cloves
1/8 tsp. ground cinnamon
• MAKES 4 CUPS •

RECIPE CARD 10

1/2 cup mayonnaise
1 T. milk
1 T. vinegar or lemon juice
1/2 tsp. sugar
1/4 tsp. salt
1/8 tsp. pepper
1 medium head cabbage, shredded
1 small green pepper, minced
1 large celery stalk, chopped
1 large carrot, shredded
2 T. minced onion
1/8 tsp. paprika
• MAKES 8 SERVINGS •

RECIPE CARD 11

1 cup mayonnaise
1/4 cup lemon juice
1 lb. red apples, diced
2 cups thinly sliced celery
1 cup chopped walnuts
1 cup dark seedless raisins
lettuce leaves
• MAKES 8 SERVINGS •

RECIPE CARD 12

1 8-oz. package noodles
1/4 cup butter, melted
1/4 cup grated Parmesan cheese
2 T. half-and-half
1/4 tsp. salt
1/8 tsp. pepper
• *MAKES 8 SERVINGS* •

RECIPE CARD 13

1 lb. ground beef
1 small onion, diced
2 cloves garlic, minced
2 1/2 cups canned tomatoes
1 can (12-oz.) tomato paste
1 T. sugar
1 1/2 tsp. salt
1/2 tsp. each oregano and thyme
1 bay leaf
1 12-oz. package of wide noodles
1 lb. Ricotta cheese
1 lb. Mozzarella cheese, shredded
• *MAKES 8 SERVINGS* •

RECIPE CARD 14

1 cup butter or margarine
4 squares unsweetened chocolate
2 cups sugar
4 eggs
1 cup all-purpose flour
1 tsp. vanilla extract
1/2 tsp. salt
2 cups chopped nuts
• *MAKES 24 SERVINGS* •

RECIPE CARD 15

sugar
1 3/4 cups all-purpose flour
1/2 cup shortening
1/3 cup milk
1 egg
1 T. baking powder
1 tsp. grated lemon peel
1/3 tsp. salt
2 pints strawberries
butter or margarine, softened
1 cup heavy cream, whipped
• *MAKES 8 SERVINGS* •

RECIPE CARD 16

3 cups bran
1 cup buttermilk
1/3 cup soft shortening
1/2 cup brown sugar
1 egg
1 cup all-purpose flour
1 tsp. baking powder
1/2 tsp. soda
1 tsp. salt
• MAKES 12 SERVINGS •

RECIPE CARD 17

4 large potatoes, grated
1 small onion, grated
2 eggs, well beaten
1/4 cup milk
2 tsp. salt
1/8 tsp. pepper
1/3 cup all-purpose flour
1/3 cup salad oil
• MAKES 16 SERVINGS •

RECIPE CARD 18

1 egg, beaten
1 cup buttermilk
1/2 cup all-purpose flour
1 1/4 cup corn meal
2 T. sugar
3 tsp. baking powder
1/4 tsp. soda
1 tsp. salt
3 T. shortening
• MAKES 10 SERVINGS •

RECIPE CARD 19

1 1/2 lb. lean pork shoulder, cut in strips
2 1/2 cups canned pineapple chunks
1/4 cup brown sugar
2 T. cornstarch
1/4 cup vinegar
3 T. soy sauce
1 small green pepper, cut in strips
1/4 cup thinly sliced onion
• MAKES 6 SERVINGS •

RECIPE CARD 20

1 1/3 cups confectioners' sugar
1 cup cake flour
1 1/2 cups egg whites, at room temp.
(12 to 14 egg whites)
1 1/2 tsp. cream of tartar
1 1/2 tsp. vanilla extract
1/4 tsp. salt
1/4 tsp. almond extract
1 cup sugar
• *MAKES 12 SERVINGS* •

RECIPE CARD 21

3 lb. loin ribs
lemon slices
1/2 cup chopped onion
2 T. brown sugar
1 T. paprika
1 tsp. salt
1 tsp. dry mustard
1/4 tsp. chili powder
2 T. Worcestershire sauce
1/4 cup vinegar
1 cup tomato juice
1/4 cup catsup
1/2 cup water
• *MAKES 3-4 SERVINGS* •

RECIPE CARD 22

1 1/2 lb. fresh shrimp
3 slices bacon, cut up
1 1/2 cups chopped onion
1/2 cup chopped green pepper
3 T tomato paste
1 T. paprika
1/4 cup chopped parsley
1 1/2 tsp. leaf thyme
1/2 tsp salt
1/4 tsp. cayenne pepper
2 1-lb. can tomatoes
3 cups cooked rice
1/2 lb. ham, diced
• *MAKES 8 SERVINGS* •

RECIPE CARD 23

1 cup sugar
1/2 cup light corn syrup
1/4 tsp. salt
1/4 cup water
1 cup shelled raw peanuts
2 T. butter or margarine
1 tsp. baking soda
• *MAKES 1 POUND* •

RECIPE CARD 24

PROJECT 17 Get out your party hats, noise makers, and confetti to celebrate some wacky holidays!

RE THE SAME OLD holidays getting a little ho-hum? Do you need some fresh and lively annual events to look forward to for a change? Well, here's your chance to put some zip into your dreary, day-in, day-out calendar and make some previously "blah" days a cause for celebration.

You have a choice of two activity cards, each one listing some unusual but authentic holidays and events. Choose one of the cards and complete these tasks:

- Discover when during the year each of the special days or weeks is celebrated. Note the source of your information.
- Write a short paragraph describing a good way to celebrate each special occasion you have identified.

BONUS: Devise your own calendar, highlighting your discoveries and including any other holidays you wish.

HAPPY NEW YEAR!

ACTIVITY CARD 1

When can you celebrate . . .

1. National Adopt-a-Cat Month
2. Sadie Hawkins Day
3. Fun Mail Week
4. Smile Power Day
5. National Rollerskating Week
6. Dr. Seuss's Birthday
7. National Failure's Day
8. National Freedom Day
9. National Pig Day
10. National Employ the Handicapped Week
11. National Baked Bean Month
12. Trivia Day
13. International Children's Book Day
14. Mickey Mouse's Birthday
15. National Clean Off Your Desk Day
16. National Ding-A-Ling Day
17. Garfield's Birthday
18. Correct Posture Month
19. Homemade Bread Day
20. "Wrong Way" Corrigan Day
21. National Humor Month
22. National Popcorn Poppin' Month
23. National Handwriting Day
24. Statue of Liberty's Birthday
25. Limerick Day
26. Potato Lover's Month

HAPPY NEW YEAR!

ACTIVITY CARD 2

When can you celebrate . . .

1. Johnny Appleseed Day
2. Singing Telegram Birthday
3. National Disc-Jockey Day
4. Teacher "Thank You" Week
5. White Cane Safety Day
6. Volunteer Fireman Day
7. National Grouch Day
8. Golden Spike Day
9. National Goof-Off Day
10. National Aviation Day
11. Human Rights Day
12. A Friend in Need Is a Friend Indeed Day
13. National Hot Dog Month
14. World Hello Day
15. Ancestor Appreciation Day
16. Pooh Day
17. National Inventor's Day
18. National Clown Week
19. Arbor Day
20. National Peanut Month
21. Passenger Pigeon Watchers Annual Count
22. Susan B. Antony Day
23. National Nothing Day
24. International Lefthanders' Day
25. Donald Duck's Birthday
26. Pioneer Day

PROJECT 18 Calling all business tycoons and Wall Street wizards! Do you know the mark of a successful company?

BIG BUSINESS

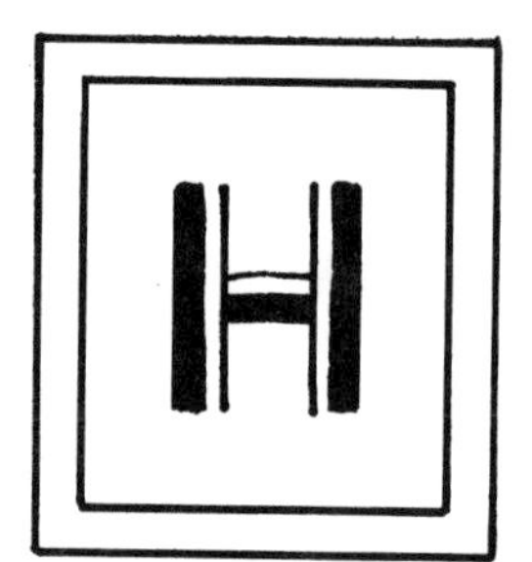

AVING AN EASILY recognized symbol, logotype,* or slogan can mean the difference between success and failure for a company trying to promote its business or product. Many of us don't think about these symbols and how important they are—or how familiar they have become to us through national advertising.

This activity gives you four different chances to observe the power of advertising at work. Choose at least two of the activity cards and complete the tasks described on the card.

* When a business chooses one particular style of lettering for the name of a product or for the company name, that particular style is called the company's **logotype.**

BIG BUSINESS ACTIVITY CARD 1

Sometimes animals are used as symbols to represent a business or a specific product. For example, you have probably seen the racing dog that appears on all Greyhound buses.

Your challenge is to find a business or a product that is represented by each of the following animals. If what you name is a product, you must also name the company that makes the product.

1. Dog (a breed besides greyhound)
2. Cat
3. Deer
4. Rabbit
5. Horse
6. Cow or bull
7. Tiger
8. Lion
9. Rooster
10. Kangaroo
11. Kiwi
12. Peacock
13. Koala
14. Giraffe
15. Penguin

BIG BUSINESS

ACTIVITY CARD 2

What product, business, or organization has used each of these slogans? Try to identify at least 15. Call yourself a real tycoon if you can get them all!

1. Don't leave home without it.
2. When you care enough to send the very best.
3. Fly the friendly skies.
4. Breakfast of champions.
5. Adventure in moving.
6. We bring good things to life.
7. Driving to be the best.
8. The right choice.
9. Making your world a little easier.
10. In business . . . for business.
11. Engineered like no other car in the world.
12. Tomorrow's technology at your touch.
13. Get a piece of the rock.
14. You're in good hands.
15. We're fighting for your life.
16. Ideas at work.
17. It's a good time for the great taste.
18. The first name in first aid.
19. You can't beat the experience.
20. The great American shoestore.
21. Helping pets live longer, healthier lives.
22. Get more for your life.
23. Better things for better living.
24. It's a matter of life . . . and breath.

BIG BUSINESS

ACTIVITY CARD 3

Many businesses choose a very special style of lettering that they always use for their company name or for a certain product. Often the initial letter or letters are formed into a special design that becomes the company's logo. For example, you've probably seen the McDonald's logo—a big M designed as a pair of "golden arches."

Your challenge: to find a distinct business logo for each letter of the alphabet. You may not be able to find them all, but find as many as you can. Trace your findings. For each letter-logo, be sure to record the name of the company or product it represents.

For each type of business listed below, name a particular one that has a distinctive symbol or logo. Trace or redraw the symbol and record the name of the organization that uses it.

1. a clothing manufacturer
2. an appliance manufacturer
3. a TV or stereo manufacturer
4. a computer company
5. a manufacturer of toys or games
6. a packager of spices or seasonings
7. an oil company
8. an airline
9. a manufacturer of breakfast cereals
10. a national credit card
11. a non profit organization
12. a hotel chain
13. a shipping company
14. a publisher
15. a recording company

PROJECT 19 If you can tell the difference between Tweedledum and Tweedledee, this one's for you!

SIX OF ONE

Half dozen of the other

THERE ARE MANY words that people use interchangeably although in fact the words mean two different things. We get confused because the words have similar meanings—so similar that we never know or never can remember the difference between them.

Choose at least a dozen of the word pairs in this activity and research to answer these questions:

- How are the two items different?
- What characteristic do the two items have in common?

Be sure to record your sources of information.

1\.

camel
dromedary

2\.

stalactite
stalagmite

3\.

understudy
standby

4\.

antiperspirant
deodorant

5.

hail

sleet

6.

sweet potato

YAM

7.

cement

concrete

8.

flotsam

jetsam

9.

anteater

aardvark

10.

puppet

marionette

11.

donkey

mule

12.

mole

vole

13.

hay
straw

14.

tuba
sousaphone

15.

horn
antler

16.

bog
swamp

PROJECT 20 It's a whatchamacallit . . . a gizmo . . .
a doohickey . . . a thingumajig!

It's On the Tip of My Tongue!

THE WORLD is full of familiar objects whose names we don't know or can't easily remember. You probably have your own word to use when you don't know the real one . . . something like "doomaflatchy." It's fun to say a word like that—but it's also fun to see the stunned look on someone else's face when you use the RIGHT word for some little gadget that no one else knows what to call.

Choose one of the activity cards and see how many special names you can discover as you complete the tasks.

IT'S ON THE TIP OF MY TONGUE! ACTIVITY CARD 1

What's the special name for these items?

1. The hard tips on the ends of a shoelace.
2. The metal band that holds the eraser on a wooden pencil.
3. The rope that is used to raise a flag up the flagpole.
4. The part of a hammer that is used to pull out nails.
5. The little part that connects the two blades of a pair of scissors.
6. The area on a baseball bat that connects with the ball when you hit a home run.
7. The part of an automatic dishwasher that rotates, squirting water onto the dishes.
8. The loop that you tuck the end of the belt through after buckling it.
9. The part of a safety pin that you tuck the point into.
10. The section of an airplane where the passengers sit.
11. The middle pedal on a piano.
12. The section of a shoe's sole between the ball of the foot and the heel.
13. The part of a hot air balloon that holds the hot air.
14. The number 5 pin in bowling.
15. The part of an iron that gets hot.
16. The triangular piece of a sundial that creates a shadow.
17. The part of an umbrella that shields you from the rain.
18. The bottom-most part of a sailboat, which usually contains ballast.
19. The metal loop that supports the shade on a lamp.
20. The part of a stapler that holds the staples.

IT'S ON THE TIP OF MY TONGUE! ACTIVITY CARD 2

Choose two of the items below. Draw a simple picture or diagram of each item and name its parts.

1. HOT AIR BALLOON (name at least 12 parts)
2. MATCHBOOK (name at least 7 parts)
3. SLED (name at least 10 parts)
4. WOODEN CLOTHESPIN (name at least 6 parts)
5. VIOLIN (name at least 10 parts)
6. ICE SKATE (name at least 8 parts)
7. CAMERA (name at least 10 parts)
8. FLOWER (name at least 8 parts)
9. CASTLE (name at least 12 parts)
10. BULLDOZER (name at least 10 parts)

PROJECT 21 Here's history with a twist . . . Can you imagine life before these inventions?

It Was A Very Good Year

HEN DID KIDS first enjoy stretching Silly Putty? or squeezing a teddy bear? or letting M&M's melt in their mouths, not in their hands? It wasn't so very long ago that none of these items existed. You may think it's a perfectly ordinary experience to wiggle cherry Jell-O on your spoon, seeing how hard you can shake it without having it end up in your lap. And you probably don't find anything unusual about struggling with a stubborn zipper that has you held captive inside your winter coat. But once upon a time, those events would have seemed quite strange, because the items in question had not yet been invented.

Choose one of the two activity cards and see how much "consumer history" you can learn. Whichever card you select, complete these two tasks:

- Discover the year when each article or product was first invented or first became available.
- To demonstrate the results of your research, create an illustrated time line depicting the information you have uncovered.

IT WAS A VERY GOOD YEAR | ACTIVITY CARD 1

When did these familiar items first arrive on the scene?

1. TEDDY BEAR
2. POP-UP ELECTRIC TOASTER
3. KLEENEX
4. PARKING METER
5. MONOPOLY
6. NYLON TOOTHBRUSH
7. ZIPPER
8. ROLLER SKATES
9. SCOTCH BRAND TAPE
10. TAB-TOP CAN
11. POGO STICK
12. TYPEWRITER
13. BALL POINT PEN
14. THERMOS BOTTLE
15. RAGGEDY ANN
16. BOTTLE CAP
17. FRISBEE
18. BIKINI
19. RUBBER BANDS
20. SILLY PUTTY
21. SHOPPING CART
22. CELLOPHANE
23. SCRABBLE
24. LEVI JEANS
25. AEROSOL VALVE
26. HULA HOOP
27. WRISTWATCH
28. BAND-AIDS
29. TOOTHPASTE TUBE
30. NEON SIGN
31. FERRIS WHEEL
32. BARBED WIRE
33. TRAFFIC LIGHT
34. COLOR FILM
35. FLUSH TOILET
36. CASH REGISTER
37. XEROX MACHINE
38. CHRISTMAS CARD

BONUS: Which of the above items are trademarked names?

IT WAS A VERY GOOD YEAR

ACTIVITY CARD 2

When did these brand-name snacks and foods first come on the market?

1. MORTON SALT
2. OREO COOKIES
3. WONDER BREAD
4. TOOTSIE ROLL
5. TWINKIES
6. HERSHEY KISSES
7. COCA-COLA
8. LIPTON TEA
9. ESKIMO PIE
10. RICE KRISPIES
11. SNICKERS CANDY BAR
12. COCO PUFFS
13. KELLOGG'S CORN FLAKES
14. SKIPPY PEANUT BUTTER
15. 7-UP
16. BABY RUTH CANDY BAR
17. RITZ CRACKERS
18. HIRES ROOT BEER
19. SHREDDED WHEAT
20. AUNT JEMIMA PANCAKE MIX
21. MILKY WAY CANDY BAR
22. DANNON YOGURT
23. POPSICLE
24. JELL-O
25. SUGAR FROSTED FLAKES
26. LIFE SAVERS
27. CAMPBELL'S CHICKEN NOODLE SOUP
28. HERSHEY BAR
29. ANIMAL CRACKERS
30. LOG CABIN SYRUP
31. CRACKER JACK
32. THOMAS' ENGLISH MUFFINS
33. M&M'S
34. FRITO-LAY CORN CHIPS
35. QUAKER OATS
36. BUTTERFINGER CANDY BAR
37. DR. PEPPER
38. REESE'S PIECES

BONUS: What is the name of the company who markets each of these products?

PROJECT 22 What hour was the clock striking as history was made?

HISTORY IS HIGHLIGHTED by certain great events, and part of learning history is learning the dates when those events occurred. For example, you probably know that the Declaration of Independence was adopted by the Continental Congress in 1776. If you are really up on your dates, you know that it was approved on July 4. But taking it one step further, do you know what *time of day* it was approved? That's harder, but with a little research you might be able to find at least the approximate hour.

This is your challenge:

- Choose one of the activity cards.
- Discover, for at least 12 of the events listed on the activity card, the time of day when they occurred. (Find the *local* time where the event took place.)
- After concluding your research, create a visual display that lists the events chronologically *by hour* within a 24-hour period, starting just after midnight.

Be sure to note the sources of your information.

HANDS OF TIME ACTIVITY CARD 1

These historical events all took place before 1920. At what time of day did each event occur?

1. September 2, 1666: The Great Fire of London begins.
2. October 21, 1805: British Admirial Horatio Nelson is shot at the Battle of Trafalgar.
3. October 25, 1854: The Charge of the Light Brigade begins at the Battle of Balaklava.
4. April 9, 1865: General Robert E. Lee surrenders at the Appomattox Courthouse, marking the end of the Civil War.
5. April 14, 1865: John Wilkes Booth assassinates President Abraham Lincoln at Ford's Theater, Washington.
6. July 14, 1865: English mountain climber Edward Whymper is the first to reach the summit of the Matterhorn.
7. August 15, 1870: The final link of transcontinental railroad track is laid at Strasburg, Colorado.
8. October 8, 1871: The Great Chicago Fire starts.
9. October 21, 1879: Thomas Edison's first successful incandescent electric lamp starts to burn.
10. March 31, 1889: The Eiffel Tower officially opens in Paris.
11. September 10, 1897: George Smith, a London taxi driver, becomes the first convicted drunk driver.
12. September 6, 1901: President William McKinley is assassinated in Buffalo, New York.
13. December 17, 1903: The first airplane flight, by Orville Wright at Kittyhawk, North Carolina, lasts 12 seconds.
14. April 18, 1906: The great San Francisco earthquake starts, lasting 55 seconds.
15. May 7, 1915: The Lusitania is sunk by German U-boat torpedoes.
16. March 31, 1918: The first daylight savings time in the United States is instituted.

HANDS OF TIME

ACTIVITY CARD 2

At what time of day did these events occur?

1. May 20, 1927: Charles Lindbergh departs from New York to attempt the first solo transatlantic flight.
2. May 21, 1927: Charles Lindbergh lands at LeBourget airfield in Paris, his flight a success.
3. May 25, 1935: Jesse Owens breaks or matches the first of six world records in a track meet in Ann Arbor, Michigan.
4. May 6, 1937: The Hindenburg explodes at Lakehurst, New Jersey.
5. September 3, 1939: British prime minister Neville Chamberlain declares war on Germany.
6. May 26, 1940: Operation Dynamo, the evacuation of trapped Allied troops from the beaches of Dunkerque, France, begins.
7. July 1, 1941: WNBT in New York broadcasts the first television commercial, advertising Bulova watches; it lasts 20 seconds.
8. December 7, 1941: Japanese attack on Pearl Harbor begins.
9. June 5, 1944: BBC radio transmits signal to French underground that D-Day is "on."
10. January 17, 1950: Alarm goes off at Brink's headquarters in Boston, Massachusetts, signaling the greatest bank robbery in U.S. history.
11. April 12, 1961: Yuri Gagarin blasts off in first successful manned space flight.
12. February 10, 1962: First spy exchange in the Cold War takes place as downed U-2 pilot Francis Gary Powers is swapped for Soviet agent Rudolf Abel.
13. November 22, 1963: President John F. Kennedy is assassinated in Dallas, Texas.
14. July 20, 1969: Mankind first lands on the moon.
15. August 9, 1974: Richard Nixon resigns as president after the Watergate scandal.
16. January 28, 1986: The space shuttle Challenger explodes.

PROJECT 23 Anyone can be stumped by difficult questions, but here's your chance to be stumped by "cinchy" ones!

IT'S A CINCH (isn't it?)

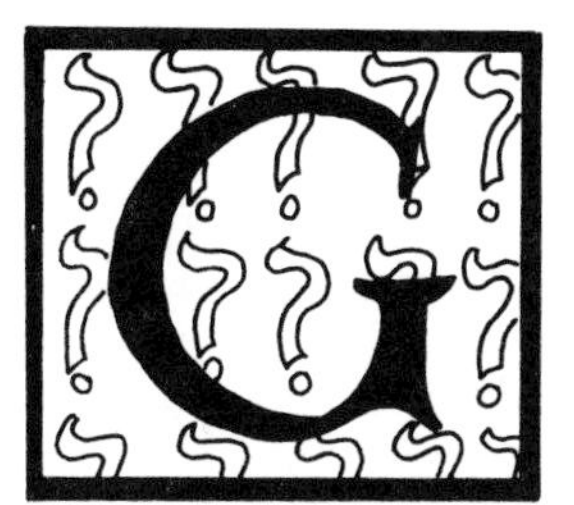

GROUCHO MARX had an old-time television quiz and comedy program called "You Bet Your Life." On occasion he would ask absurdly simple questions, such as " Who was buried in Grant's tomb?" or "What color is an orange?" The point was to give contestants the chance to win a few easy dollars. His ulterior motive, though, was to milk chuckles from the audience. And it worked because the contestants, expecting difficult questions, were often stumped or tongue-tied when such obvious questions were thrown at them.

You're not playing "You Bet Your Life" here, but you do have a chance to see how well you can handle the "cinch" questions on the activity card. Be careful! The answers look obvious—but are they really?

IT'S A CINCH (ISN'T IT?) ACTIVITY CARD

1. How long did the Hundred Year's War last?
2. What is a camel's hair brush made of?
3. Can the fifth wheel on a tractor-trailer ever go flat?
4. Which of the world's people devised the Turkish bath?
5. If you order Welsh rabbit for dinner, what will you be served?
6. In what month do Russians celebrate the October Revolution?
7. What animal is pictured on the buffalo nickel?
8. What are moleskin trousers made of?
9. From what country do we get India ink?
10. Where do Chinese gooseberries come from?
11. What animal were the Canary Islands named after?
12. In what country did French-fried potatoes originate?
13. During what time of year does Shakespeare's play, "A Midsummer Night's Dream," take place?
14. What is Queen Anne's lace made of?
15. In the original fairy tale, what was Cinderella's slipper made of?

PROJECT 24 Can you save these letters from the dead letter file?

POST OFFICE

HAVE YOU EVER dreamed of sneaking into the back rooms of the post office to see what happens to your letters after you slip them into the slot that says "Local" or "Out of Town"? You might be surprised at how efficient the operation is—as long as people address their envelopes properly. Unfortunately, people don't always do that.

If you accept the challenge of this activity, you will know a little what it feels like to be a befuddled postal worker dealing with problem mailings. You will have a handful of envelopes with incomplete addresses. Choose 10 of these envelopes to work on. Rather than tossing them into the "Return to Sender" bin, do some research to discover the intended destination. It's above and beyond the call of duty, but the senders will thank you!

HINT: The destinations are well-known organizations, landmarks, tourist attractions, or company headquarters.

ENVELOPE 1

POSTAGE

1750 East Boulder Street
Colorado Springs, CO 80909

ENVELOPE 2

POSTAGE

19 North Square
Boston, MA 02113

ENVELOPE 3

POSTAGE

1 Lincoln Plaza
New York, NY 10022

ENVELOPE 4

POSTAGE

500 South Buena Vista Street
Burbank, CA 91521

ENVELOPE 5

Independence Avenue at 6th Street, SW
Washington, DC 20560

ENVELOPE 6

1260 Avenue of the Americas
New York, NY 10020

ENVELOPE 7

Commerce and House Streets
San Antonio, TX 78205

ENVELOPE 8

E. 42nd Street and First Avenue
New York, NY 10017

ENVELOPE 9
POSTAGE
Box 3485
Williamsport, PA 17701
ENVELOPE 10
POSTAGE
1155 Battery Street
San Francisco, CA 94106
ENVELOPE 11
POSTAGE
20525 Mariana Drive
Cupertino, CA 95014
ENVELOPE 12
POSTAGE
6th and Chestnut Streets
Philadelphia, PA 19106

ENVELOPE 13

301 North Avenue, NW
Atlanta, GA 30313

ENVELOPE 14

320 W. Colfax Avenue
Denver, CO 80204

ENVELOPE 15

The American Road
Dearborn, MI 48126

ENVELOPE 16

206-208 Hill Street
Hannibal, MO 63401

PROJECT 25 If you're a clock-watcher in school, then this one's for you!

Tick...Tick...Tick I

EACH POCKET WATCH pictured in this activity describes three events that take differing amounts of time. What the watches *don't* tell you is how long that period of time is. Your challenge is to discover these unknown times through research.

You have two tasks in order to complete this activity in a timely manner:

- Choose at least four of the watches and find the approximate time for each item listed.
- For each timepiece you have chosen to research, add the three times to determine the total time represented on that watch.

HINT: The items on each pocket watch will all be measured in similar units of time, either seconds, minutes, hours, days, or years. That makes your second task easier.

TICK . . . TICK . . . TICK . . . I
POCKET WATCH 1
• Time it takes to see Charlie Chaplin's movie "The Tramp"
• Time it takes to play a half in a soccer game
• Time it takes to prepare Minute Rice
FACT-FINDERS COPYRIGHT ©1987 BY DALE SEYMOUR PUBLICATIONS
TICK . . . TICK . . . TICK . . . I
POCKET WATCH 2
•Time it takes to fly between London and Los Angeles
•Length of time Thomas Edison's first lightbulb burned
•Length of a "day" on the planet Neptune
FACT-FINDERS COPYRIGHT ©1987 BY DALE SEYMOUR PUBLICATIONS

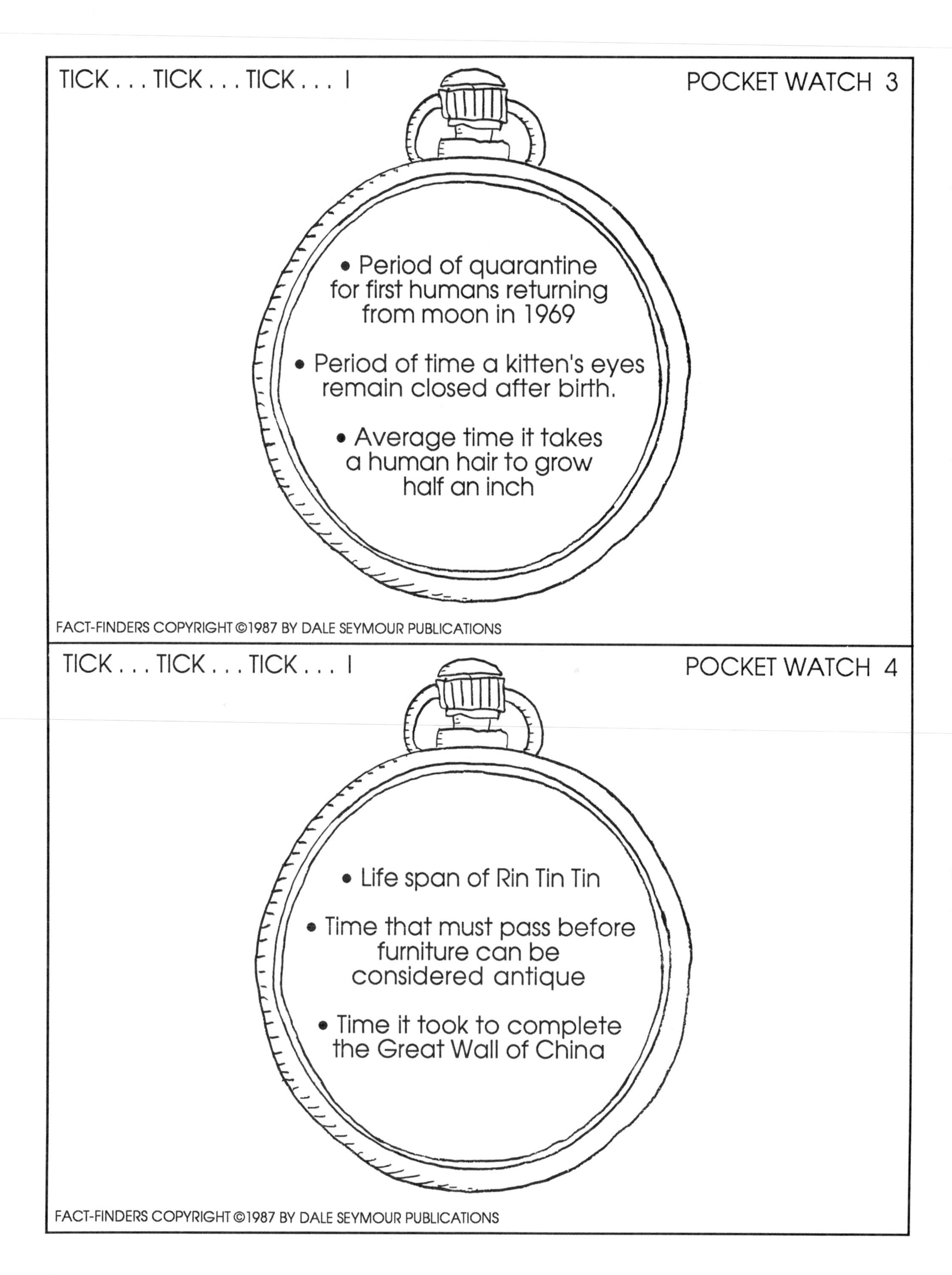
TICK . . . TICK . . . TICK . . . I
POCKET WATCH 3
• Period of quarantine for first humans returning from moon in 1969
• Period of time a kitten's eyes remain closed after birth.
• Average time it takes a human hair to grow half an inch
FACT-FINDERS COPYRIGHT ©1987 BY DALE SEYMOUR PUBLICATIONS
TICK . . . TICK . . . TICK . . . I
POCKET WATCH 4
• Life span of Rin Tin Tin
• Time that must pass before furniture can be considered antique
• Time it took to complete the Great Wall of China
FACT-FINDERS COPYRIGHT ©1987 BY DALE SEYMOUR PUBLICATIONS

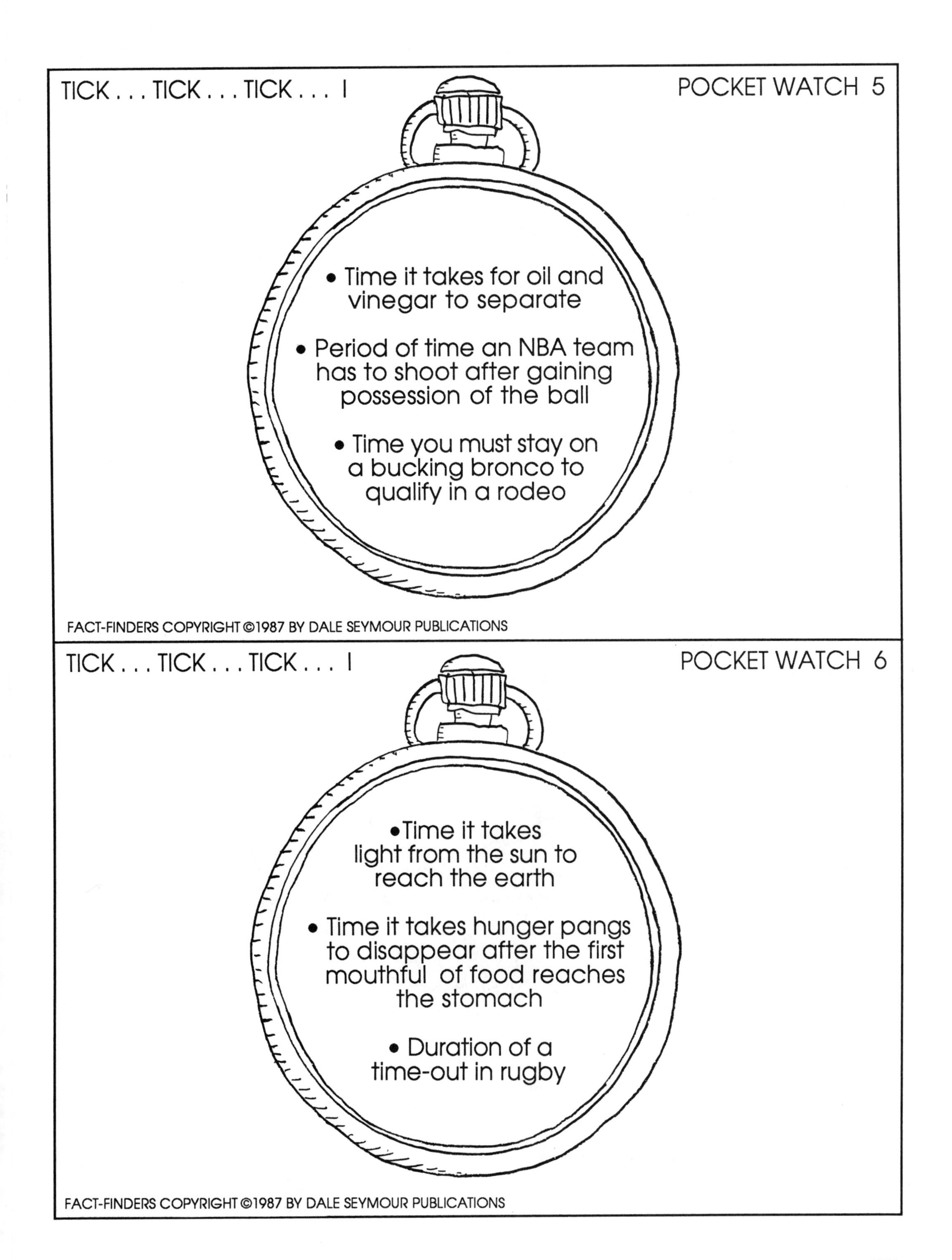
TICK . . . TICK . . . TICK . . . I
POCKET WATCH 5
• Time it takes for oil and vinegar to separate
• Period of time an NBA team has to shoot after gaining possession of the ball
• Time you must stay on a bucking bronco to qualify in a rodeo
FACT-FINDERS COPYRIGHT ©1987 BY DALE SEYMOUR PUBLICATIONS
TICK . . . TICK . . . TICK . . . I
POCKET WATCH 6
•Time it takes light from the sun to reach the earth
• Time it takes hunger pangs to disappear after the first mouthful of food reaches the stomach
• Duration of a time-out in rugby
FACT-FINDERS COPYRIGHT ©1987 BY DALE SEYMOUR PUBLICATIONS

PROJECT 26 Is this the sort of thing you can do time and time again?

Tick...Tick...Tick II

VEN IF YOU have already completed the first of these activities, the clock just keeps on ticking. Tick, tick, tick , tick. . . so go the seconds, the minutes, the hours, the days, the weeks, the months, the years. Your challenge is the same this time around:

- Choose at least four of the pocket watches and discover the duration of the three items listed on each one.
- Add together the three times to determine the total time for each pocket watch you have chosen.

TICK . . . TICK . . . TICK . . . II
POCKET WATCH 1
• Time it took the Titanic to sink
• Time it takes cream to rise to the top of fresh milk
• Time it takes for a Duraflame log to burn

TICK . . . TICK . . . TICK . . . II
POCKET WATCH 2
•Time it took Handel to compose "The Messiah"
• Interval of time between washings of windows of the Empire State Building
• Length of a "day "on the planet Venus

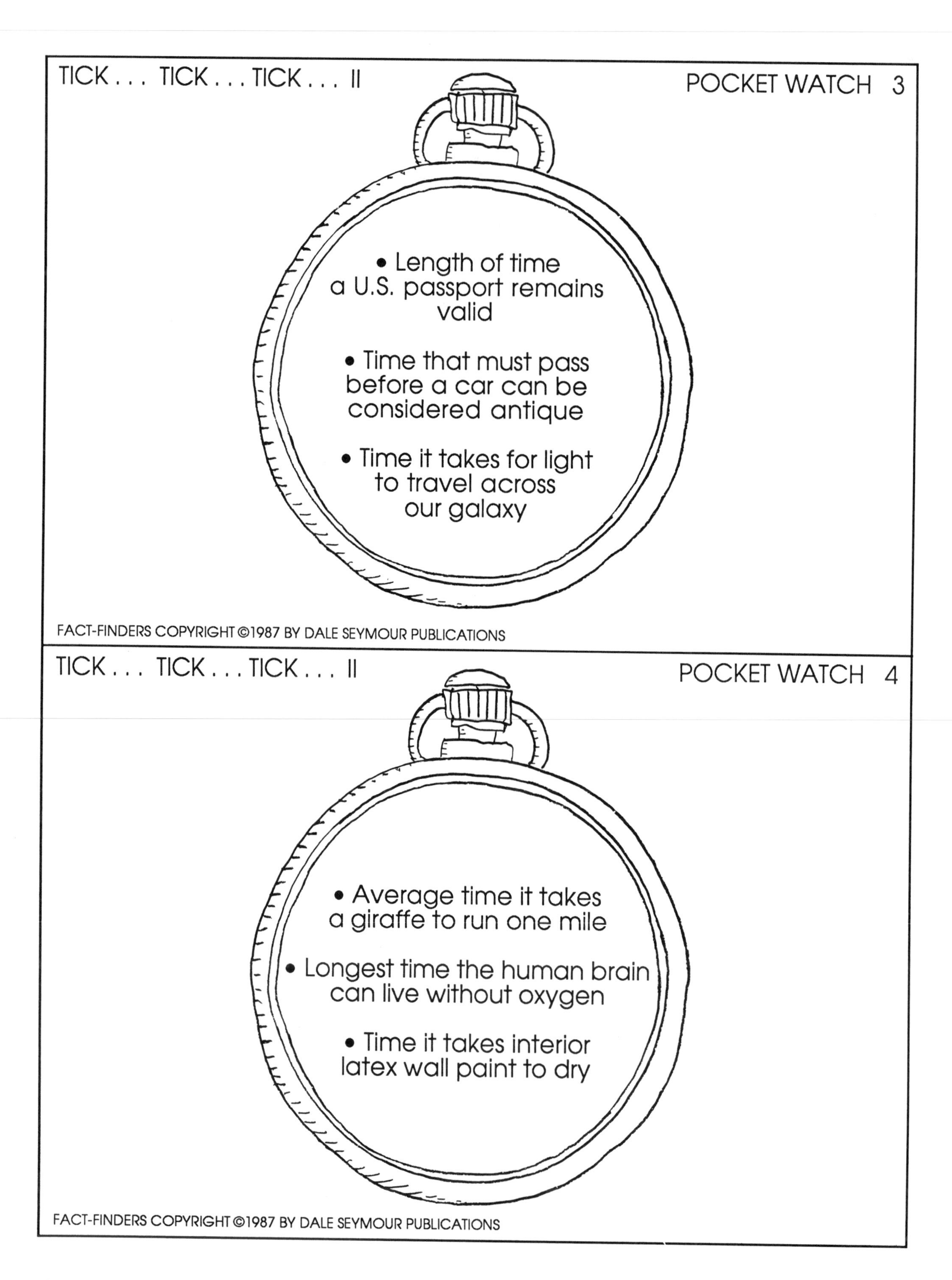
TICK . . . TICK . . . TICK . . . II
POCKET WATCH 3
• Length of time a U.S. passport remains valid
• Time that must pass before a car can be considered antique
• Time it takes for light to travel across our galaxy
FACT-FINDERS COPYRIGHT ©1987 BY DALE SEYMOUR PUBLICATIONS
TICK . . . TICK . . . TICK . . . II
POCKET WATCH 4
• Average time it takes a giraffe to run one mile
• Longest time the human brain can live without oxygen
• Time it takes interior latex wall paint to dry
FACT-FINDERS COPYRIGHT ©1987 BY DALE SEYMOUR PUBLICATIONS

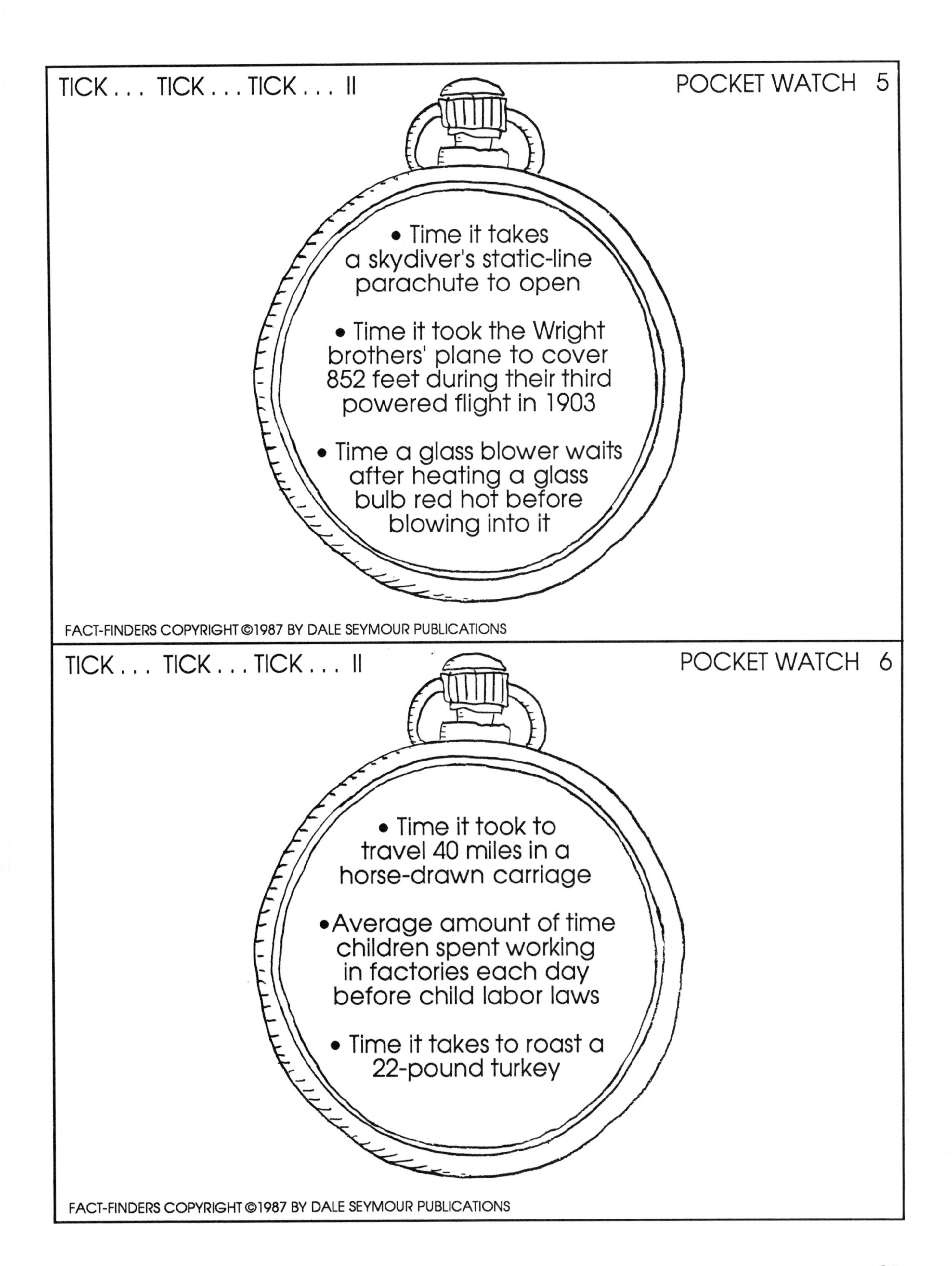
TICK . . . TICK . . . TICK . . . II
POCKET WATCH 5
• Time it takes a skydiver's static-line parachute to open
• Time it took the Wright brothers' plane to cover 852 feet during their third powered flight in 1903
• Time a glass blower waits after heating a glass bulb red hot before blowing into it
FACT-FINDERS COPYRIGHT ©1987 BY DALE SEYMOUR PUBLICATIONS
TICK . . . TICK . . . TICK . . . II
POCKET WATCH 6
• Time it took to travel 40 miles in a horse-drawn carriage
• Average amount of time children spent working in factories each day before child labor laws
• Time it takes to roast a 22-pound turkey
FACT-FINDERS COPYRIGHT ©1987 BY DALE SEYMOUR PUBLICATIONS

PROJECT 27 Snatch someone from history and plan an unforgettable itinerary for the two of you to share!

TIME MACHINE

YOU HAVE THE UNIQUE opportunity to invite one noted person from the past to visit you and the present for just two days. That's right—you have only 48 hours to entertain this historical figure and explain or demonstrate what has happened to the world since that person died.

To complete this activity, you must undertake three tasks:

- Choose one name from the list on the activity card. Research that person's life to discover why he or she was an important figure in history. Be sure to keep track of your sources.
- Devise a schedule of activities for your visitor from the past. Be sure to incorporate activities relevant to that person's interests. Of course, you will also need to introduce this person to the wonders of our modern-day world, many of which probably seem extremely common or ordinary to you—such as turning on the television or riding in an automobile.
- Finally, write a report that includes an explanation of why you chose each activity on your itinerary and a hypothesis of what your visitor's reactions would be.

TIME MACHINE

ACTIVITY CARD

Notable Historical Figures Available for a Visit

Pythagoras • Hippocrates of Cos • Mohammed

Johannes Gutenberg • Jeanne d'Arc

Nicolaus Copernicus • Ferdinand Magellan

Queen Elizabeth I • Miguel de Cervantes Saavedra

Pocahontas • Rembrandt van Rijn • Sir Christopher Wren

Johann Sebastian Bach • Catherine the Great

Abigail Adams • Tecumseh • Samuel Morse

Mary Wollstonecraft Shelley • Hans Christian Andersen

Amelia Bloomer • Lydia Estes Pinkham • Susan B. Anthony

Florence Nightingale • Louis Pasteur

Harriet Tubman • Sarah Winnemucca • Sarah Bernhardt

Nellie Bly • Marie Curie • Scott Joplin

Mohandas Gandhi • Enrico Caruso • Isadora Duncan

Helen Keller • Jim Thorpe • Anne Frank

PROJECT 28 Are you in the right state to take on this activity?

FABULOUS 50

HARDLY ANYONE in this country escapes the clutches of elementary school geography without having to learn the names and locations, and usually even the capitals, of the 50 states in the United States. Your challenge here is to take that exercise a step further and devise a system that would make learning the 50 states an enjoyable experience. Choose one of the suggestions on the activity card or use your own clever imagination to tackle this challenge.

Research one of these or come up with your own method.

1. Identify each state by a tourist attraction, either famous or odd, found within its borders.
2. Identify each state by naming—and, if possible, humming—its state song.
3. Identify each state with a bit of trivia related to it.
4. Identify each state by a famous person who was born there—maybe an athlete, an artist, a politician, a writer, a musician, a scientist, or an entertainer.
5. Identify each state by one of its towns or cities that has an unusual name.
6. Identify each state by a famous event that occurred there.
7. Identify each state by its nickname, or motto, or state bird, or state flower, or state tree.
8. Identify each state by its outline shape.
9. Identify each state by its auto license plate design.

PROJECT 29 What was the world like when you first opened your peepers?

Look Out World ~ Here I Come!

HEN YOU DECIDED to make your grand entrance on this earth of ours, what was the world like? Your challenge is to go back in time and give a detailed account of the day you were born. This "account" may take the form of a scrapbook, a newspaper, a series of taped interviews, a mini-museum, or another idea of your own choosing.

Include all the information listed on the activity card, but do not restrict your research to those topics. To get you started . . .

What did your horoscope predict the day you were born?

Was it raining cats and dogs?

How much did a Hershey's Almond Bar cost? (You say you don't like those? Well then, how about a Twix bar—or were they even around then?)

Did kids your present age play with video games or program their home computers?

What were Snoopy and the gang up to? Or Garfield?

LOOK OUT WORLD—HERE I COME! ACTIVITY CARD

Include these topics as you research the day of your birth.

1. Major news headlines
2. The weather
3. Sports news
4. Your horoscope
5. Entertainment (movies, plays, TV, radio, music)
6. Foods
7. Literature
8. Fashions
9. Popular games and toys
10. Homes and furnishing styles
11. Gadgets
12. Comics and cartoons
13. Transportation
14. Science and technology
15. Fads

HERE'S A TWIST: Instead of concentrating on yourself, research the day that one of your parents or grandparents was born. You may have to do a bit more investigating and detective work, but the results are guaranteed to be well worth the extra effort!

PROJECT 30 Calling all future astronauts . . . and don't forget to bring your scales!

Don't Tip the Scales!

GET READY FOR a space voyage to one of seven planets. Your role is Gravitational Force Expert. As you may know, each of the planets exerts a different gravitational force on objects. Therefore, something that weighs 10 pounds on earth—an armadillo, for example— would weigh less than half as much on Mars and more than twice as much on Jupiter. Your mission is a complicated one, so pay close attention:

- Choose one of the planet cards.
- Research to discover the weight, on earth, of each object listed on the planet card.
- Use the Gravitational Factor Table to determine what each item would weigh on your chosen planet.
- Give the weight (on earth and on your planet) of the following items:
  1. Your school principal or your teacher at birth
  2. The amount you can lift comfortably with no strain
  3. The 10-pin bowling ball you would use most comfortably
  4. Your own weight
  5. The weight of another object of your choice

Create a chart on which to record your findings.

DON'T TIP THE SCALES!

Gravitational Factor Table

This table gives the gravitational force on each of the planets expressed as a factor of the gravitational force on earth.

Mercury	0.38
Venus	0.90
Mars	0.38
Jupiter	2.87
Saturn	1.32
Uranus	0.93
Neptune	1.23
Pluto	unknown

DON'T TIP THE SCALES! PLANET CARD 1

Mercury

Find the weight of:

1. the largest pancake ever flipped
2. the largest strawberry ever grown
3. the average African elephant
4. the New York City telephone directory
5. R.M.S. Queen Elizabeth II
6. 20 average chickens

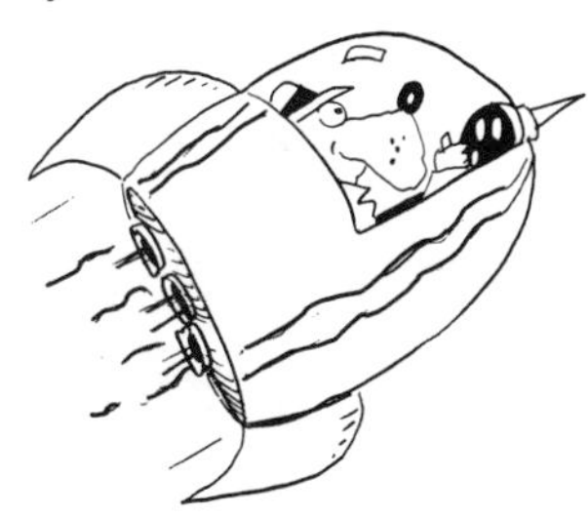

DON'T TIP THE SCALES!

PLANET CARD 2

Venus

Find the weight of:

1. the smallest bird in the world
2. the largest chocolate Easter egg ever made
3. a space shuttle, fueled for launch
4. the average polar bear
5. a bar of gold at Fort Knox
6. the average human brain

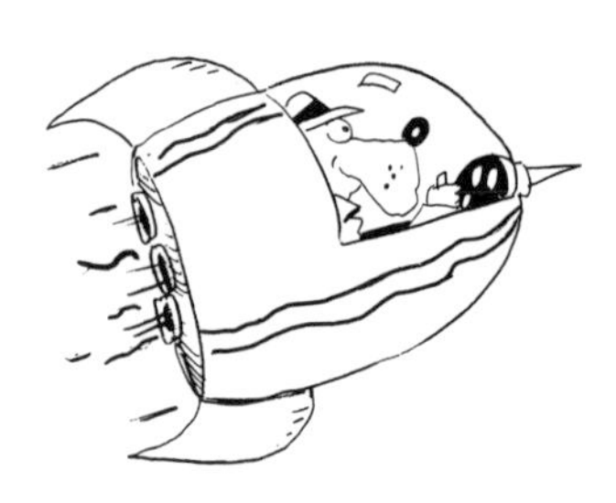

DON'T TIP THE SCALES!

PLANET CARD 3

Mars

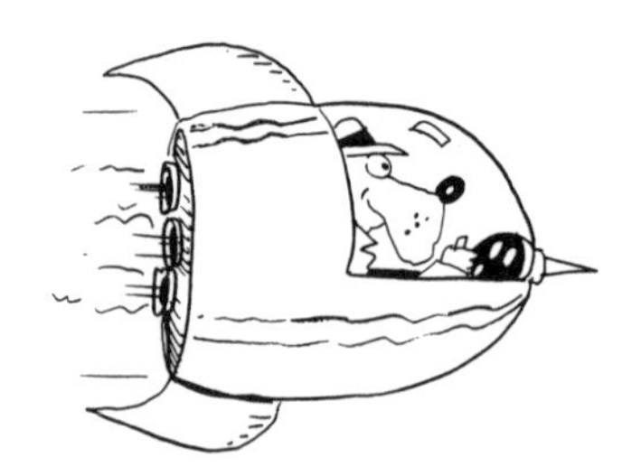

Find the weight of:

1. the largest hamburger ever grilled
2. the largest watermelon ever grown
3. the average horse
4. the largest ball of string on record
5. the average ostrich egg
6. the Statue of Liberty

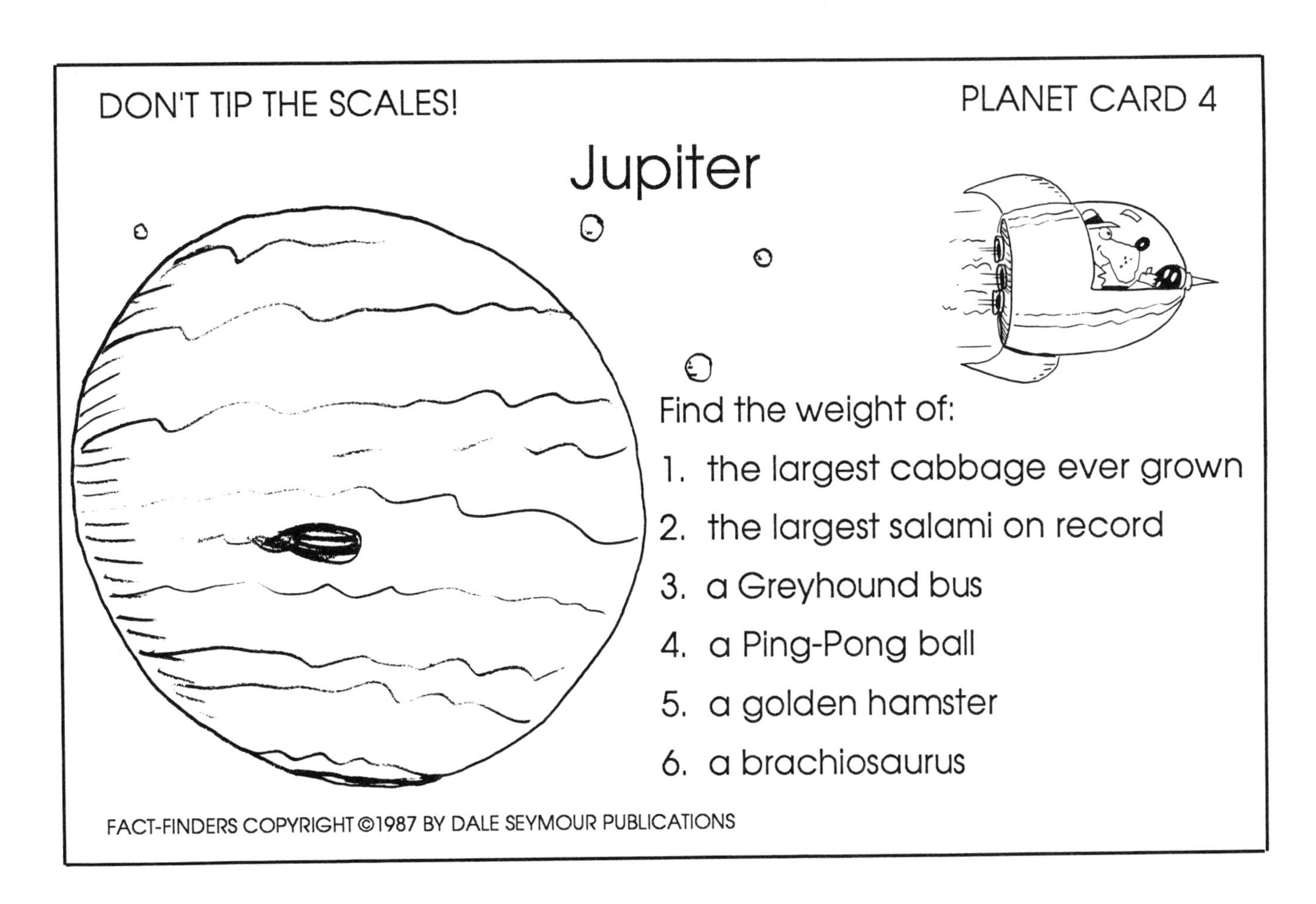

DON'T TIP THE SCALES!

PLANET CARD 4

Jupiter

Find the weight of:

1. the largest cabbage ever grown
2. the largest salami on record
3. a Greyhound bus
4. a Ping-Pong ball
5. a golden hamster
6. a brachiosaurus

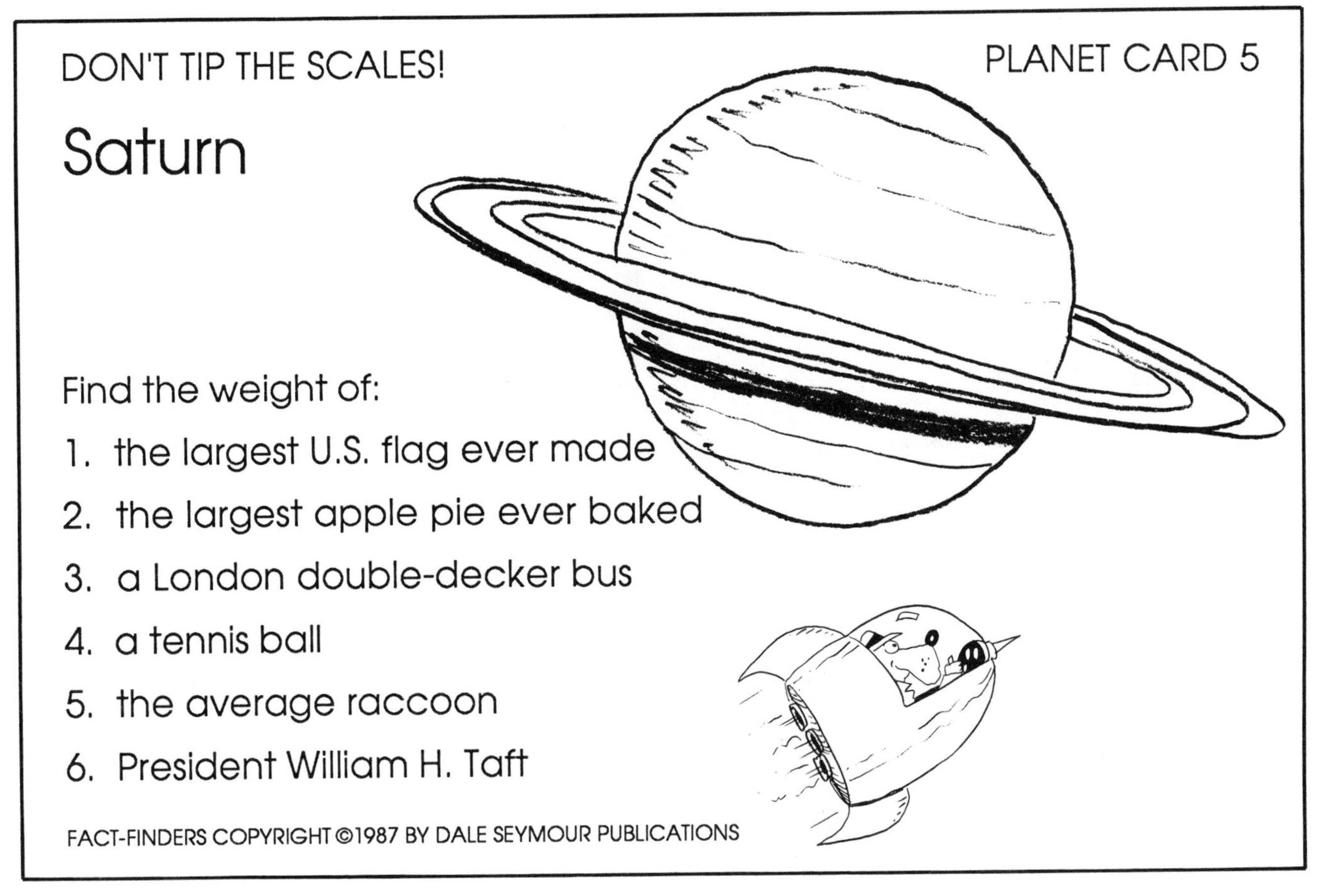

DON'T TIP THE SCALES!

PLANET CARD 5

Saturn

Find the weight of:

1. the largest U.S. flag ever made
2. the largest apple pie ever baked
3. a London double-decker bus
4. a tennis ball
5. the average raccoon
6. President William H. Taft

DON'T TIP THE SCALES! PLANET CARD 6

Uranus

Find the weight of:

1. the world's largest rodent
2. the largest radish ever grown
3. the blocks at Stonehenge
4. a baseball
5. the average cat
6. the greatest weight ever lifted by a person

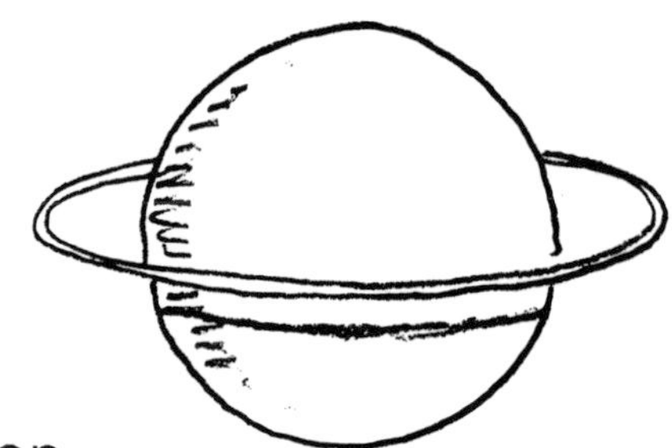

DON'T TIP THE SCALES! PLANET CARD 7

Neptune

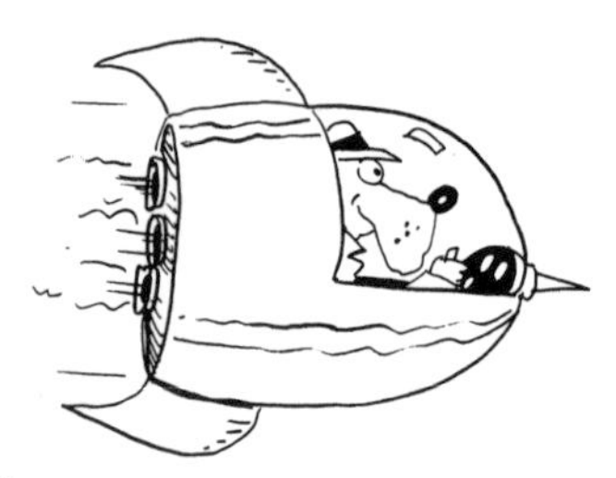

Find the weight of:

1. the largest cake ever baked
2. a brick
3. a soccer ball
4. The Wright Brothers' first plane, *Flyer I*
5. the average llama
6. a dinosaur's brain

FACT-FINDERS Answer Guide

Project 1. NEW (OLD) NAMES FOR OLD (NEW) PLACES
Sources include *The Book of Lists #1, The World Almanac and Book of Facts,* encyclopedias and world atlases.

Activity Card 1: **1.** Fort Dearborn **2.** Abyssinia **3.** Gold Coast **4.** Sandwich Islands **5.** Netherlands (or Dutch) East Indies **6.** Constantinople **7.** St. Petersburg **8.** Nyasaland **9.** South-West Africa **10.** New France **11.** Christiania **12.** Netherlands (or Dutch) Guiana **13.** Tanganyika **14.** Edo **15.** Northern Rhodesia **16.** Belgian Congo

Activity Card 2: **1.** Djakarta **2.** Belize **3.** Sri Lanka **4.** Santo Domingo **5.** Gdansk **6.** Bangladesh **7.** Taiwan **8.** Pittsburgh (Pennsylvania) **9.** Toronto **10.** Italy **11.** Albania **12.** Iran **13.** Ho Chi Minh City **14.** Thailand **15.** Volgograd **16.** Mexico City

Project 2. SHORT STUFF
Sources include *The World Almanac Book of Who, Webster's Biographical Dictionary, The Book of Lists #2,* encyclopedias.

Activity Card 1: **1.** Alan Alexander Milne, British writer most well known for Pooh books **2.** Benjamin Franklin Goodrich, U.S. tire manufacturer **3.** James Cash Penney, U.S. merchant who developed nationwide department store chain **4.** Herbert George Wells, British writer **5.** William Claude Fields, U.S. comic actor **6.** John Ronald Reuel Tolkien, British writer well known for *The Hobbit* **7.** Phillip Knight Wrigley, U.S. chewing gum manufacturer **8.** edward estlin cummings, U.S. poet, well known for his eccentric typography **9.** Phineas Taylor Barnum, U.S. showman who formed Barnum & Bailey circus **10.** Thomas Stearns Eliot, British-U.S. poet

Activity Card 2: **1.** John Chapman, U.S. conservationist who planted many apple trees in Midwest **2.** Ferdinand Morton, U.S. ragtime and jazz piano player **3.** Anna Mary Robertson, U.S. folk painter **4.** Theodor Seuss Geisel, U.S. writer and illustrator of children's books **5.** Orenthal James Simpson, U.S. football player and sportscaster **6.** Mary McCauley, U.S. Revolutionary heroine who carried water to troops in battle and fired cannon **7.** Julius Marx, U.S. comedian **8.** Phoebe Anne Oakley Mozee, U.S. sharpshooter and entertainer **9.** George Herman Ruth, U.S. baseball Hall of Fame great **10.** Claudia Alta Johnson, U.S. business woman and First Lady who championed environmental causes

Project 3. SECRET IDENTITIES
Sources include *The Book of Lists #2, The Dictionary of Misinformation,* and encyclopedias and dictionaries.

1. No, a peanut is a seed of a vine of the legume family, which includes peas and beans. **2.** No, a woolly bear is the caterpillar of the tiger moth. **3.** No, a horned toad is a small lizard. **4.** Yes, shoofly pie is a pie made of molasses and brown sugar. **5.** No, dry cleaning is not dry—it doesn't use water, but it does use other liquids, such as naphtha. **6.** Yes, the electric eel has special organs that can give severe electric shocks. **7.** No, a shooting star is a meteor. **8.** No, a geoduck (pronounced "gwee-duck") is a large burrowing clam. **9.** No, a guinea pig is a small mammal of the rat family. **10.** Yes, a cowbird is a blackbird. **11.** No, a banana tree is a tropical herb. **12.** No, coffee beans are seeds found inside a berry of a tropical shrub. **13.** Yes, breadfruit is a large tropical fruit. **14.** No, shortbread is a rich cake or cookie. **15.** No, an English horn is a reed instrument like an oboe, and it's from France. **16.** No, a lead pencil is made of wood and graphite. **17.** Yes, a beanbag is traditionally filled with dry beans, although many "beanbag chairs" are stuffed with small foam pellets instead. **18.** No, the funny bone is a spot on the elbow where the nerve can be pressed against the bone to create a sharp tingling feeling. **19.** No, a firefly is a winged beetle. **20.** Yes, a wood duck is a colorful North American duck. **21.** No, a silk worm is a moth caterpillar. **22.** No, rice paper is made from a shrubby plant of the ginseng family. **23.** No, a prairie dog is a burrowing rodent. **24.** Yes, foam rubber is rubber with air beaten into it. **25.** No, a starfish is not a fish but an echinoderm, like a sea urchin. **26.** No, a firedog is an andiron, which holds wood in a fireplace. **27.** No, the bald eagle has white feathers on its head. **28.** No, black-eyed peas (also called cowpeas) are in fact a kind of bean.

Project 4. YOU DON'T SAY!
Sources include *The Book of Lists #2, Comparisons, Guiness Book of World Records,* and encyclopedias.

NOTE: Answers for this activity will vary somewhat, depending on the source.
1. For the average grasshopper, "knee-high" would be about 1/2 inch. Figuratively, the expression means "when someone was a small child." **2.** Human skin ranges from 1/100 inch to 1/5 inch thick; figuratively, "having thin skin" means someone is sensitive and easily hurt by criticism. **3.** A horse will eat about 15 pounds of hay and 9 pounds of grain in a day; figuratively, "eats like a horse" means eating a lot. **4.** A wink happens in 1/10 of a second; figuratively, "quick as a wink" means very quickly. **5.** The common garden snail moves at 0.03 miles per hour, or just over two inches a minute; figuratively, "at a snail's pace" is very slow. **6.** The actual depth will vary, depending on the height of the person; figuratively, "up to one's neck" means nearly overwhelmed by. **7.** Natural ice over a pond or stream should be at least 4 inches thick before you try skating on it, so "thin ice" is anything less than 4 inches. Figuratively, "skating on thin ice" means someone is taking a chance, flirting with danger. **8.** A feather weighs only 0.5 gram or less; figuratively, "light as a feather" means very light. **9.** A ton of bricks is about 736 bricks; figuratively, "hit like a ton of bricks" means to affect very strongly, usually to disturb. **10.** Based on a payment of 40 cents a word, a picture would be worth $400; figuratively, the expression means that some things can be communicated more easily in a picture than by trying to describe them in words. **11.** The speed of a bullet varies from 800 to 4000 feet per second, depending on the type of gun used; figuratively, the expression simply means very fast. **12.** The worth of "a hill of beans" might be determined by estimating the yield of the bean plants in "a hill" and finding the current retail price for beans at the supermarket; figuratively, the expression means not worth much at all.

Project 5. MENAGERIE MEDLEY
Sources include *The Book of Lists #1, An Exaltation of Larks, The Complete Unabridged Super Trivia Encyclopedia, The Teacher's Book of Lists,* and various animal encyclopedias.

NOTE: Some of these answers will vary depending on the source. Students will find that much of this terminology is not absolute, and that many of the group names and animal baby names are used interchangeably.

Activity Card 1: **1.** covey **2.** cete **3.** pride **4.** pack **5.** cast **6.** flock, gaggle, skein **7.** lepe **8.** skulk **9.** sloth **10.** crash

Activity Card 2: **1.** many large animals, for example, cattle, wild horses, antelope, reindeer, elephants, water buffalo **2.** many domestic animals that move in a herd, such as sheep or goats; also many birds, such as chickens, pigeons, turkeys, seagulls, waxwings. **3.** many social insects, such as ants, bees, and termites; also mammals and birds that set up group living situations, such as beavers, rabbits, and penguins **4.** animals that move in herds, often upright rather than on all fours, such as monkeys, baboons, and kangaroos **5.** sea mammals that travel in herds, such as whales, dolphins, and seals

Activity Card 3: **1.** spat **2.** cygnet **3.** poult **4.** piglet, shoat **5.** joey **6.** gosling **7.** colt **8.** elver **9.** eyas **10.** fingerling, grilse **11.** cheeper **12.** squab

Activity Card 4: **1.** bear, lion, tiger, leopard, and sometimes fox and wolf **2.** cat, beaver, and sometimes fox **3.** dog, seal, coyote, wolf, sometimes fox **4.** cow, elephant, giraffe, rhinoceros, whale, bison, water buffalo

Project 6. MIXED-UP MATCHES
Various encyclopedias and biographical dictionaries will be useful, but the students will also need to be creative and check a variety of miscellaneous sources in finding the connections. Some of their answers may vary; accept any that show a logical connection.

1. They might be close together under title listings since both wrote books that had titles beginning with the word "Little." **2.** Jim Davis is the creator of the comic strip "Garfield" and Don Marquis wrote a column about Archy the cockroach and Mehitabel the cat; both were humorists who developed distinctive cat characters. **3.** Each was the "first" official leader of his country, Washington being the first U.S. president and MacDonald the first Canadian prime minister. **4.** Both used pseudonyms; their real names were Samuel Langhorne Clemens and Agatha Mary Clarissa Miller. **5.** Both were awarded the Nobel Peace Prize. **6.** Each was the first woman in space for her country. **7.** What they have in common is *Frankenstein.* She wrote the novel, and he played the monster in the 1931 film based on the book. **8.** Both claim the best-selling single record to date—Bing Crosby with 25 million of "White Christmas," and Bill Haley and the Comets with 25 million of "Rock Around the Clock" *(Guinness Book of World Records, 1986 Edition).* **9.** Both are famous for their voices, Blanc as the voice of many cartoon characters, including Sylvester and Tweety Bird; Tokyo Rose as a radio broadcaster of anti-U.S. propaganda in World War II. **10.** Tabei was the first woman and Hillary the first man to successfully climb Mt. Everest.

Project 7. CRAZY CONTESTS
A single good source is *The Contest Book,* but resourceful researchers will find this information in many other places as well.

NOTE: A number of these contests are common to many different areas, and may be known by slightly different names. For example, many local organizations sponsor "bed races," and local milk companies often hold "milk carton boat races." Students should be allowed considerable leeway in their answers as long as they can cite sources for them.

1. Stuttgart, Arkansas **2.** Coney Island **3.** Kenwood, California **4.** Pawtucket, Rhode Island **5.** Montpelier, Vermont **6.** Twelve Mile, Indiana **7.** Geneva, Ohio **8.** Britt, Iowa **9.** Bloomer, Wisconsin **10.** Spring Hill, Florida **11.** Wolsey, South Dakota **12.** Kelso, Washington **13.** Wellesley, Massachusetts **14.** Bedford, Pennsylvania **15.** Anchorage, Alaska **16.** Virginia Beach, Virginia **17.** Stroud, Oklahoma **18.** Spivey's Corner, North Carolina **19.** Hannibal, Missouri **20.** Carrizo Springs, Texas **21.** Virginia City, Nevada **22.** Caryville, Florida **23.** Weatherford or Paul's Valley, both in Oklahoma **24.** Sterling, Colorado **25.** Priest Lake, Idaho **26.** Pittsfield, Maine **27.** Newport, Rhode Island **28.** Yuma, Arizona **29.** Philadelphia, Pennsylvania **30.** Great Falls, Montana or Beaver, Oklahoma **31.** San Francisco, California **32.** Mackinac Island, Michigan **33.** Columbia, Tennessee **34.** Rayne, Louisiana **35.** Gurnee, Illinois **36.** Albuquerque, New Mexico **37.** Wildwood by the Sea, New Jersey **38.** Rogue River, Oregon **39.** Angels Camp, California **40.** Liberal, Kansas

Project 8. TRIVIA TRICKSTERS I
Sources include *Fascinating Facts, Encyclopedia Brown's Record Book of Weird and Wonderful Facts, You're Dumber in the Summer, The Complete Unabridged Super Trivia Encyclopedia,* and *Far-Out Facts.*

1. The Dead Sea is very salty—25% salt—which makes the water very heavy, so a person's body is very buoyant. **2.** This claims to be the shortest sentence in the English language that includes every letter of the alphabet. **3.** The purpose of the magnet is to attract nails, staples, tools, tacks, wire, and so forth that the cow may pick up while grazing. **4.** Flamingos get their color from their food, tiny blue-green algae that turn pink during digestion. **5.** Tug-of-war, backstroke (swimming), and rowing (or crew). **6.** Ms. Gooding played the organ during their home games. **7.** The flavors in order are lemon, cherry, orange, lime, pineapple, cherry, lemon, lime, pineapple, cherry, and orange. This order is always the same. **8.** The first word was "Houston." The first sentence was, "That's one small step for man, one giant leap for mankind." **9.** Yes, tall office buildings are designed to sway as much as 3 feet. **10.** The plants get moisture from fog that rolls in from the Pacific Ocean and from snowmelt from nearby mountains.

Project 9. TRIVIA TRICKSTERS II
Suggested sources are the same as for the preceding activity.

1. Although it is sometimes reported that the Great Wall of China is visible from the moon, in fact that is a myth (according to NASA Media Services in Houston); *no* man-made structures can be seen. However, astronauts orbiting 400-500 miles out have reported seeing the Great Wall as well as canals, long freeways and rail lines, and the wakes of ships at sea. At night, the lights of large population centers are visible from orbit. **2.** Quito's extreme elevation, 9300 feet above sea level, moderates the tropical climate. **3.** People digging through the sand could find fresh-water fish in underground streams. **4.** Shivering increases muscular action and therefore body temperature. **5.** On June 16, 1976, rain flooded the grounds around the stadium so that players and officials were prevented from getting to the Astrodome. **6.** This custom originated in the Northeast, and red paint was the cheapest. **7.** The earth gains weight from meteoric dust that falls to the earth, as much as 100,000 pounds every year. **8.** It takes time for light to travel through space. When we look out into space and see a distant object shining, we are looking through time as well as space, because the light we see was generated a long time ago. For example, if the object we see is a billion light years away, then the light that we are seeing left that object a billion years ago. Theoretically, we may be seeing light today that dates back to the beginning of the universe. **9.** Ducks have glands near the tail that secrete an oil. They rub this over their feathers, and oil repels water. This is how they are able to keep from getting water-logged. **10.** A porcupine has more than 30,000 quills, and each quill is hollow. All the air in those quills makes them very buoyant in the water.

Project 10. SUPER SLEUTH I
Although some dictionaries offer a minimal etymology for some words, it is hoped that this activity will lead students to discover the many fascinating books available on word origins. These include *101 Words and How They Began, Dictionary of Word and Phrase Origins, What's Behind the Word, Words, Horsefeathers and Other Curious Words,* and *Word Origins and Their Romantic Stories.*

NOTE: Many sources differ on the etymology of words. In some cases, legends have grown up around certain words. Clever though they may be, these legends may have little basis in fact. This is part of what makes word study so intriguing. Students are encouraged to share whatever information they find, and to realize that probably no single source is "the last word" in etymology.

1. *Spaghetti* actually means "little strings." **2.** *Clue* originally meant "a ball of thread." This is why one is said to "unravel" the clues of a mystery. **3.** *Clodhopper* originated in early England as a term for the peasantry. Farmers, who traveled by foot, had to step or "hop" across clods of plowed earth, unlike the upper classes, who traveled by carriage or horse. Hence, the peasants were "clod-hoppers." **4.** *Diaper* was originally a kind of pure white silk fabric used to make priests' robes, and later was used to describe the finest and whitest cloth made, often used for tablecloths. After the mechanical loom was invented, weavers began producing a cheap cotton material that some called diaper because it resembled table linen. This cloth was so inexpensive that people used it for all manner of everyday things—tablecloths, dustcloths, and even babies' pants. Eventually, the word came to mean only the cloth used for babies, and now it refers to the garment itself, regardless of material. **5.** *Bride* comes from an Old German word meaning "to cook" or "to make broth." One of the first jobs of a new wife, or bride, was to make the broths for the daily meals. **6.** *Slap-stick* comedy is named after an actual stick used in Italian comedies in the 16th century to slap the rumps of stooges. **7.** *Coward* comes from the Latin word *cauda,* meaning "tail." It was used to describe what one saw when a frightened animal "turned tail" and ran away. **8.** *Denim* is a cloth originally made in the town of Nimes, France. In England it was described by the phrase "de Nimes," meaning "from Nimes," and was eventually shortened to denim. **9.** In Old Dutch, and later in Old English, an ell was a measure of length, like a foot, except that an ell was the distance from the tip of the middle finger to the bend of the arm. The Dutch word for bend is *Boog,* which turned to *bow* in Old English. Hence, *Ell-bow.* **10.** According to one source, *kangaroo* means "I don't know" in an Aborigine tongue. It is said that when a visitor to Australia asked a native the name of this unusual hopping creature, the

Aborigine replied "Kangaroo," and that became the English word for the beast. **11.** In France, corduroy was the cloth used to make hunting clothes for royal families. The French word *corde* means "cord, rope, or line," which refers to the appearance of the fabric. *Du roi* means "of the king." Hence, corduroy means "corded fabric of the king." **12.** In some northern English dialects, the term *lolly* means tongue, from the word *loll,* meaning "to hang the tongue out." It's easy to imagine how this term came to be linked to the familiar lump of candy on a stick. **13.** *Carousel* comes from the Italian word *carosello,* meaning "little chariot." **14.** *Pretzel* comes from the German *brezel,* from the Latin *brachiatus,* meaning "having branches like arms." **15.** *Hippopotamus* means "river horse," from the Greek words *hippos* (horse) and *potamus* (river). **16.** *Doodle* may derive from the German word *dudeln,* meaning "to play the bagpipes." The implication is that playing this instrument is a frivolous waste of time, much like scribbling aimlessly on scraps of paper. **17.** In early sailing days, the only holes in the side of a ship were the ports for guns—or *portholes*. Later, when similar holes were added as windows to admit light and air to the quarters below deck, they were given the same name. **18.** *Canter* probably is a shortened form of "Canterbury," and refers to the gait used by the horses (a slow and gentle gallop) as people made the pilgrimage to Canterbury cathedral. **19.** In 490 BC, the Athenians defeated the Persians in battle at Marathon, and a Greek runner carried the news to Athens, 26.6 miles away. Today the special races called *marathons,* which are 26.6 miles long, honor that ancient runner. **20.** The weight of precious gems is measured in carats. The word comes from *carob,* the Arabic name for a tree with seed pods that weigh almost exactly the same. These seeds were used in the ancient African markets to balance the scales used for weighing gems. **21.** *Genuine* comes from the Latin word *gegenere,* "to beget" or "to be born." In an old custom, the father of a newborn child placed the infant on his knee to announce his acceptance of the baby as his real child. Hence, genuine has come to mean "real, not counterfeit." **22.** The Mandarin Chinese word meaning "to fry" or "to cook" is *ch'ao.* The word came to this country with the Chinese laborers in the 1850's who worked laying tracks for the railroad. *Chow* is now a slang word for food; it also appears in the Americanism *chow mein,* meaning literally "cooked noodles." **23.** Mummy comes from the Arabic word *mum,* the name of the liquid wax used by ancient Egyptians to embalm bodies in preparation for burial. **24.** There is a contested legend about the origin of this word, which claims that a theater manager in Dublin bet that he could bring a new word into the English language in 48 hours. He then had street children chalk these four meaningless letters, *q-u-i-z*, on walls all over the city. When people asked what it meant, they were told it was a practical joke. The first meaning of *quiz* was practical joke; later it took on other meanings—trick, puzzle, and test of knowledge.

Project 11. SUPER SLEUTH II
Sources are the same as for the preceding activity.

1. *Sabotage* originated with French strikers in the 19th century, who organized planned, calculated nuisances to drive employers to distraction. They took the word from children who annoyed adults by clacking their sabots (wooden shoes) together until the clickety-clack drove them mad. **2.** *Purple* is from the Latin *purpura,* from the Greek *porphyra,* which was the name of a shellfish from which a dark bluish-red dye was obtained by boiling its shell. **3.** *Pumpernickel* is from the French, *pain* (bread) *pour Nicoli* (for Nicoli, the name of Napoleon's horse). It was coined by Napoleon's troops, who complained that although they were poorly fed, there was always food for the commander's horse. **4.** *Khaki* is the Hindustani word for "dirt"; it came to mean the fabric used for uniforms when British soldiers in India tried to camouflage their white uniforms by rolling in the dirt. **5.** *Scuba* originated as an acronym for "Self-Contained Underwater Breathing Apparatus." **6.** In the British Isles, the word *pip* meant "apple seed" and later the seed of any fruit, such as oranges and lemons. The expression "I'll squeeze you till the pips squeak" meant to squeeze someone like a fruit until the seeds could be heard to complain. *Pipsqueak* came to mean someone who complained under pressure, and later anyone small who whined about troubles. **7.** *Umbrella* is from the Latin *umbra,* meaning shade. Umbrellas were first used to make shade, protecting the user from the heat of the sun (especially in the tropics). The umbrella was first used for protection against rain in London in 1750. **8.** *Tulip* comes from the Turkish word *tulbend,* meaning "turban." People once thought that the flower looked like the turban Turkish men wore. **9.** Long ago, English judges put on a special cap—a thinking cap—while sentencing a criminal, as a sign that they had thought carefully about the punishment. Now "to put on one's thinking cap" simply means to think about something very carefully. **10.** *Dandelion* is from the French, *dent de lion,* or "tooth of a lion." It was supposed that the jagged leaf of the plant looked like lion's teeth. **11.** The Chinese made a spicy sauce they called *ketsiap;* Dutch traders borrowed the sauce and called it *ketjap;* the English modified the sauce to suit their taste and called it *ketchup.* **12.** *Mustache* comes from the Greek *mystax,* meaning "upper lip," where mustaches are found. **13.** *Muscles* derive from the Latin word *mus,* "mouse," and *musculus,* "little mouse." Apparently when people saw muscles moving in arms and legs, they thought it looked like little mice moving around under the skin. **14.** *Cereal* comes from the ancient Roman goddess *Ceres,* protector of crops such as corn and wheat, from which cereal is made. **15.** *Eggs Benedict* are named after a Mr. and Mrs. Le Grand Benedict, who suggested the recipe to a hotel chef. **16.** In the 19th century when the polka was the dance rage, there was a custom of naming articles of dress after the popular dance of the day. So there was "polka gauze," and "polka hats," and fabric with *polka dots.* **17.** *Perfume* comes from the Latin, *per* meaning "by means of" and *fumus* meaning "smoke." It refers to the fact that incense was burned during religious ceremonies to conceal the odor of the sacrifice—"by means of sweet-smelling smoke." **18.** *Racket* comes from the Arabic word *rahat,* meaning "palm of the hand." All of our racket sports derive from an original game in which a ball was hit with the palm. **19.** Because the inexpensive seats on benches at a baseball field were always in the sun, the wood became lighter, or bleached out. Hence the name *bleachers.* **20.** Salary comes from the Latin *salarium,* meaning "salt ration." In the Roman army, soldiers were given all their food and clothing, but they were not paid money except for a few coins to buy important things, like salt (*sal* in Latin). In English salary came to mean "money paid for doing a regular job." **21.** The first marshmallows were made from the root of a plant, named *malua* in Latin, that grew in the marshes (*mariscus* in Latin) along Mediterranean shores. They were called *marismalua*— translated to *marshmallow* in English. **22.** Pan was a troublemaking Greek god whose sudden appearance caused terror and made people run screaming. Our word *panic* comes from his name. **23.** *Barber* is from the Latin word *barba,* meaning "beard"—which barbers cut or trim. **24.** *Coco* comes from the Portuguese and means "bogeyman with a little grinning face." It refers to the little "face" we see on one end of the nut of that particular palm tree.

Project 12. NUTTY NUMBERS
Sources include *The Complete Unabridged Super Trivia Encyclopedia, Guinness Book of World Records,* and countless other almanacs, encyclopedias, and reference books.

Activity Card 1: **1.** 336 dimples **2.** 16 ones **3.** 2,130 games **4.** 38 lines, 19 vertical and 19 horizontal **5.** 4 players **6.** 56 signers **7.** 16 moons (subject to change) **8.** $1500 **9.** 108 stitches **10.** 6005 miles **11.** 40 feet **12.** 28 years, 2 months, 19 days

Activity Card 2: **1.** 29,028 feet **2.** 44.4 carats **3.** 46 strings **4.** 4,160 miles **5.** $5,368,709.12 **6.** 32 faces **7.** 36 spokes **8.** 4,260 feet **9.** 7 feet 11 inches **10.** 50 years **11.** 85 decibels **12.** 100,000 hairs

Project 13. ODD JOBS
Sources include the *Dictionary of Occupational Titles, Words, The Book of Jargon, The Book of Lists #2,* and dictionaries.

Activity Card 1. **1.** In a piano factory, assembles and fits interior parts, or the "belly," of pianos. **2.** In a railroad yard, couples and uncouples cars being moved; rides the cars and turns hand brakes to control speed. **3.** In a clock factory, straightens and screws into place the "feet" on watch and clock dials during assembly. **4.** In a candy factory, tends the machine that mixes the ingredients used in processing chocolate kisses. **5.** Arranges and mounts letters, logos, and numbers on paper backing to make signs and displays. **6.** Assistant to the gaffer on a movie production set, the gaffer being the chief electrician, responsible for the lighting. **7.** Road worker who lays the reflective, ceramic buttons or tiles on roads and in parking lots. **8.** In boot and shoe manufacturing, treats the lasts (shoe molds) with a chalky preparation to prevent them from sticking to the shoes. **9.** Also in a shoe factory, applies liquid coating to shoe parts to prevent squeaking. **10.** In a printing plant, works on the machine that staples ("saddle stitches") magazines, comic books, and catalogs, looking to save any that are missing staples or have wrinkled, creased, or dog-eared pages. **11.** Cuts, assembles, and joins materials to form the cushioned seat of a saddle. **12.** In a garment factory, ties together bundles of garment parts after they are cut and before they are sewed together. **13.** Tends the machine that stitches rooted hair onto doll's heads. **14.** Sorts and packs hay before it is bundled into disk form for use as an archery target. **15.** In a sawmill, feeds rough lumber into a machine to cut off the uneven edges and to cut it into boards of set widths. **16.** Repairs the metal "mother" that is used to press phonograph records, removing dirt and particles from the sound-track grooves.

Activity Card 2. **1.** Analyzes handwriting to appraise personal characteristics. **2.** A professional whistler. **3.** Analyzes secret coding systems and decodes messages for military, political, or law enforcement agencies. **4.** Practices the art of fine handwriting and hand-lettering. **5.** Studies the life processes of fungi (such as mushrooms) to discover those useful to medicine, agriculture, and industry. **6.** Composes text for opera or musical play, putting words to music composed by someone else. **7.** Lays out and matches aerial photos taken in sequence for use in making maps. **8.** Designs and prepares artistic food arrangements for buffets. **9.** Loads and unloads ship cargos. **10.** Cuts and fits window glass. **11.** Assembles and repairs oilfield machinery and equipment (derricks, etc.). **12.** Prepares detailed drawings for such diverse items as satellites, bridges, skyscrapers, and gardens, based on specifications made by scientists, engineers, architects, and designers. **13.** Collects and stores records and documents of historical significance. **14.** Designs, makes, and sells fashionable, usually custom-made clothing. **15.** A rope walker. **16.** In the medical profession, an ear-nose-throat specialist.

Project 14. HOT OFF THE PRESS
***Webster's Ninth New Collegiate Dictionary* gives in parentheses, after each entry word, the date when it is thought to have entered the language. Additional sources include *I Hear America Talking* and *Listening to America*.**

There are numerous possible answers, each reflecting some new invention or technology, or social change. For example: babysitter, aircondition, nylon, pizza, antiperspirant, brainwashing, artificial intelligence, hatchback, floppy disc, word processor, food processor, subcompact, press secretary, anorexic, condo, bikini, chopper (for helicopter), aerobics, laser, and so forth.

Project 15. COLLECTOR'S EDITION
One good single source for this information is *Words*. Answers can also be found in dictionaries, encyclopedias, and miscellaneous reference books.

Activity Card 1: **1.** keys **2.** picture postcards **3.** stamps other than postage stamps **4.** cheese labels **5.** coins **6.** postage stamps **7.** matchbooks **8.** envelopes with postmarks **9.** recipes

Activity Card 2: **1.** arctophilist **2.** exonoumiast **3.** oologist **4.** philographer **5.** plangonologist **6.** conchologist **7.** lepidopterologist **8.** hostelaphile **9.** discophile

Project 16. WHAT'S COOKING?
Cookbooks are the obvious sources for this information.

1. chestnut stuffing for poultry **2.** chili con carne **3.** chicken salad **4.** Boston baked beans **5.** gazpacho **6.** eggs Benedict **7.** quiche Lorraine **8.** meat loaf **9.** ratatouille **10.** applesauce **11.** coleslaw **12.** Waldorf salad **13.** fettucine Alfredo **14.** lasagne **15.** brownies **16.** strawberry shortcake **17.** bran muffins **18.** potato pancakes **19.** cornbread **20.** sweet and sour pork **21.** angel food cake **22.** barbecued ribs **23.** shrimp jambalaya **24.** peanut brittle

Project 17. HAPPY NEW YEAR!
Sources include *Chase's Annual Events, Amazing Days,* and almanacs.

Activity Card 1: **1.** June **2.** Varies somewhat; usually a Saturday in November. **3.** second week in March **4.** June 15 **5.** last week in September **6.** March 2 **7.** August 15 **8.** February 1 **9.** March 1 **10.** first week in October **11.** July **12.** January 4 **13.** April 2 **14.** November 18 **15.** third Monday in January **16.** December 12 **17.** June 19 **18.** May **19.** November 17 **20.** July 17 **21.** April **22.** October **23.** January 23 **24.** October 28 **25.** May 12 **26.** February

Activity Card 2: **1.** March 11 **2.** July 28 **3.** last Friday in April **4.** first week in June **5.** October 15 **6.** second Sunday in January **7.** third Monday in October **8.** May 10 **9.** March 22 **10.** August 19 (Orville Wright's birthday) **11.** December 10 **12.** June 15 **13.** July **14.** November 21 **15.** September 27 **16.** January 18 **17.** February 11 **18.** first week in August **19.** varies from state to state; often the last Friday in April **20.** March **21.** September 1 **22.** February 15 **23.** January 16 (first celebrated 1973) **24.** August 13 **25.** June 9 **26.** varies; July 24 in Utah, second Monday in October in South Dakota

Project 18. BIG BUSINESS
The best sources for this activity are magazines of all different kinds, and in some cases the yellow pages of the telephone directory.

Activity Card 1: Answers may vary. Possibilities include the following. **1.** the RCA Victor dog , the Hush Puppies dog, or the Buster Brown dog **2.** the Crave catfood cat **3.** the Hartford Life Insurance or the John Deere farm equipment stag **4.** the Volkswagen Rabbit or the Trix cereal rabbit **5.** the Ford Mustang or the Jordache jeans horse **6.** Elsie the Borden cow or the Merrill Lynch bull **7.** the Exxon tiger or the Kellogg's Sugar Frosted Flakes tiger **8.** the MGM lion **9.** the Kellogg's corn flakes rooster **10.** the Pocket Books kangaroo **11.** Kiwi shoe polish **12.** the NBC peacock **13.** the Qantas airlines koala **14.** the Toys-R-Us giraffe **15.** Penguin books

Activity Card 2: **1.** American Express card **2.** Hallmark cards **3.** United Airlines **4.** Wheaties **5.** U-Haul rental trucks and trailers **6.** General Electric **7.** Chrysler **8.** AT&T **9.** Whirlpool appliances **10.** Tandy computers **11.** Mercedes Benz **12.** Smith Corona **13.** Prudential Life Insurance **14.** Allstate Insurance **15.** American Heart Association **16.** Black & Decker **17.** McDonald's **18.** Johnson & Johnson **19.** Pan Am **20.** Kinney Shoes **21.** Ralston Purina **22.** Sears **23.** DuPont **24.** American Lung Association

Activity Cards 3 and 4: Answers will vary.

Project 19. SIX OF ONE, HALF DOZEN OF THE OTHER
One useful source is the *Simon and Schuster Book of Facts and Fallacies,* although a dictionary and encyclopedia can also provide all the information needed for this activity.

1. *Camel* generally refers to the Bactrian camel; it has two humps, amazing strength, and not much speed. A dromedary is an Arabian camel; it has one hump and shows unusual speed; it has been bred for riding. Both are large, some would say ugly, ruminant mammals of the desert used for carrying loads. **2.** Stalactites hang from the ceiling and stalagmites stick up from the floor; both are calcite deposits found in caverns. **3.** In theater jargon, an understudy is an actor who learns a small role in a particular play, or sometimes several small roles, and is available at the theater to jump in whenever one of those cast members is ill. A standby is also a backup actor who backs up the big star; rather than waiting backstage, this person need only be available by phone. Both are "second choice" actors. **4.** An antiperspirant reduces the amount of perspiration or sweat; a deodorant does not affect quantity of perspiration but masks the odor and inhibits odor-causing bacteria. Both are personal hygiene products. **5.** Hail forms as ice in the clouds and then drops to earth, whereas sleet starts falling as rain and freezes on the way down. Both are cold, wet, miserable weather conditions to be caught outside in. **6.** Sweet potatos are yellow and dry when cooked, whereas yams are red-orange and moist. Both are roots commonly served as vegetables, especially in Southern cooking. **7.** Cement is a fine, gray powder made by burning clay and limestone; it's mixed with sand and water for small patch jobs. Concrete is cement mixed with gravel and pieces of stone for added strength. Both are building materials. **8.** Flotsam is the wreckage of a boat or its cargo, found floating on the sea; jetsam is anything that people throw overboard from a ship in distress in order to lighten the cargo and maybe save the ship. Both are found after shipwrecks, sometimes washed ashore. **9.** An anteater is any of several tropical American mammals with long snouts and long sticky tongues; it is a term commonly used for the South American ant bear. An aardvark is an African mammal with a piglike snout, long ears, a long, sticky tongue, and strong claws. Both feed exclusively on ants and termites. **10.** A puppet is manipulated from below by hand or by a rod or stick. Marionettes are manipulated from above by wires or strings or rods. Both are a form of moving doll designed to amuse children. **11.** A donkey is a long-eared, smaller cousin of the horse; a mule is the offspring of a male donkey and a female horse. Mules are usually sterile and do not have babies. Both donkeys and mules are related to horses and are used as beasts of burden. **12.** Moles are insectivores; they usually live alone and eat insects and grubs they find as they burrow through the earth. Voles are rodents; they look like mice, live in colonies, and generally eat seeds and grain. **13.** Hay is grass and clover that has been cut and dried; it is used for feeding livestock. Straw is stalks of wheat, oat, or other grain—what's left when the grain heads have been removed; it is used for bedding in barns. Both are often baled or stacked for use on farms throughout the year. **14.** A tuba is a brass instrument with its bell opening straight up; a tuba player sits and holds the tuba in his or her lap. The sousaphone, developed by John Philip Sousa for marching bands, is a tuba that has been partly "unwound" with the bell facing front, making it easier to carry. Both are brass musical instruments. **15.** Horns have a bony core and they keep growing throughout an animal's entire life. Antlers are made of hardened skin material; they are shed each year and a new pair is grown. Many antlers form branches as they grow; horns never branch, although they come in a wide variety of shapes. Both are used by animals for self-protection and in fighting over mates. **16.** A bog may contain plants and grasses, but not trees. A swamp has trees. Both are areas of very wet, spongy land.

Project 20. IT'S ON THE TIP OF MY TONGUE!
Two good sources for this activity are *What's What* and *The Facts on File Visual Dictionary*.

Activity Card 1: 1. aglets or tags **2.** ferrule **3.** halyard **4.** claw **5.** pivot **6.** barrel, meat, hitting area **7.** spray arm **8.** keeper **9.** head, cap, guard, sheath, or clasp **10.** fuselage **11.** sustaining pedal, sostenuto pedal **12.** shank **13.** envelope, bag **14.** kingpin **15.** soleplate **16.** gnomon **17.** canopy, fabric **18.** keel **19.** harp **20.** channel

Activity Card 2: Answers will vary.

Project 21. IT WAS A VERY GOOD YEAR
Students may find some differing answers for this activity. Accept any as long as the students can cite a source. Possible sources include *The First of Everything, The People's Almanac, The People's Almanac #2, The Book of Lists #2, The Book of Firsts,* and *Famous First Facts, 4th edition.*

Activity Card 1: 1. 1902 **2.** 1918 **3.** 1924 **4.** 1935 **5.** 1933 **6.** 1938 **7.** 1893 **8.** 1759, 1863 **9.** 1925 **10.** 1963 **11.** 1919 **12.** 1867 **13.** 1938 **14.** 1892 **15.** 1918 **16.** 1892 **17.** 1957 **18.** 1946 **19.** 1820, 1845 **20.** 1949 **21.** 1937 **22.** 1908 **23.** 1952 **24.** 1873 **25.** 1949 **26.** 1958 **27.** 1790 **28.** 1920 **29.** 1892 **30.** 1910 **31.** 1893 **32.** 1874 **33.** 1926 **34.** 1935 **35.** 1775 **36.** 1879 **37.** 1938 **38.** 1843

Activity Card 2: 1. 1885 **2.** 1911 **3.** 1927 **4.** 1896 **5.** 1930 **6.** 1907 **7.** 1886 **8.** 1890 **9.** 1921 **10.** 1928 **11.** 1930 **12.** 1958 **13.** 1906 **14.** 1932 **15.** 1933 **16.** 1921 **17.** 1933 **18.** 1886 **19.** 1893 **20.** 1889 **21.** 1923 **22.** 1942 **23.** 1924 **24.** 1896 **25.** 1952 **26.** 1913 **27.** 1933 **28.** 1894 **29.** 1902 **30.** 1887 **31.** 1896 **32.** 1880 **33.** 1940 **34.** 1932 **35.** 1901 **36.** 1923 **37.** 1886 **38.** 1978

Project 22. HANDS OF TIME I
Sources include *People's Almanac #3*, *Chase's Annual Events*, and *The Book of Firsts*.

Activity Card 1: **1.** 1:00 AM **2.** 1:25 PM **3.** 11:00 AM **4.** 1:30 PM **5.** 10:15 PM **6.** 1:40 PM **7.** 2:53 PM **8.** 8:30 PM **9.** 1:30 AM **10.** 2:05 PM **11.** 12:45 PM **12.** 4:07 PM **13.** 10:35 AM **14.** 5:12 AM **15.** shortly after 2 PM **16.** 2:00 AM

Activity Card 2: **1.** 7:52 AM **2.** 10:22 PM **3.** 3:15 PM **4.** 7:25 PM **5.** 11:15 AM **6.** 6:57 PM **7.** 10:10 PM **8.** 7:52 AM **9.** 9:15 PM **10.** 7:27 PM **11.** 9:07 AM **12.** 8:52 AM **13.** 12:30 PM **14.** 4:17 PM **15.** 12:00 PM **16.** 11:39 AM

Project 23. IT'S A CINCH (ISN'T IT?)
Sources include *People's Almanac #3*, *The Dictionary of Misinformation*, and dictionaries.

1. 116 years, from 1337 to 1453 **2.** generally, from squirrel's hair **3.** No, it's a metal coupling. **4.** the Romans **5.** a dish made of melted cheese, milk, and seasonings on toast **6.** November **7.** a bison (the term "buffalo" should be reserved for African and Asian water buffaloes) **8.** cotton **9.** China **10.** New Zealand **11.** dogs (Latin name *Canariae Insulae*, meaning "Island of the Dogs") **12.** Belgium **13.** spring **14.** petals— it's a flower. **15.** fur

Project 24. POST OFFICE
Sources include *The Address Book* and *The National Directory of Addresses and Telephone Numbers*, as well as telephone directories, travel guides, and chamber of commerce brochures for the cities named on the envelopes. Students will have to do some creative sleuthing, using the "guess and check" approach to problem solving, to identify the addresses.

1. U.S. Olympic Committee **2.** Paul Revere House **3.** Children's Television Workshop **4.** Walt Disney Productions **5.** Smithsonian Institution, National Air and Space Museum **6.** Radio City Music Hall **7.** the Alamo **8.** United Nations **9.** Little League Baseball **10.** Levi Strauss Company **11.** Apple Computer **12.** Independence Hall **13.** Coca-Cola Company **14.** U.S. Mint **15.** Ford Motor Company **16.** Mark Twain boyhood home and museum

Project 25. TICK . . . TICK . . . TICK . . . I
One source for nearly all the information in this activity and the next one is *Durations: The Encyclopedia of How Long Things Take*. Otherwise, students will need to explore a wide variety of resources. Some of the answers will vary somewhat, depending on the source.

Watch 1. 26 minutes, 45 minutes, and 5 minutes **Watch 2.** 9 hours, 45 hours, and 16 hours **Watch 3.** 21days, 4 days, 30 days **Watch 4.** 14 years, 100 years, 1800 years **Watch 5.** 20 seconds, 24 seconds, and 8 seconds **Watch 6.** 8 minutes, 20 minutes, and 3 minutes

Project 26. TICK . . . TICK . . . TICK . . . II
See source notes for preceding activity.

Watch 1. 4 hours, 12 hours, and 3 hours **Watch 2.** 25 days, 15 days, and 225 days **Watch 3.** 5 years, 25 years, 100,000 years **Watch 4.** 2 minutes, 7 minutes, and 30 minutes **Watch 5.** 6 seconds, 59 seconds, and 2 seconds **Watch 6.** 8 hours, 16 hours, and $6^1/_4$ hours

Project 27. TIME MACHINE.
Answers will vary.

Project 28. FABULOUS 50.
Answers will vary.

Project 29. LOOK OUT WORLD—HERE I COME! Answers will vary.

Project 30. DON'T TIP THE SCALES!
Sources for the weights listed on the cards include *Guinness Book of World Records* and *Comparisons*. The weights given in this answer key may change with new editions of *Guinness* and may differ if the students use other resources. Any reasonable answers are acceptable as long as students note their sources.

Planet card 1. Earth weights (to be multiplied by 0.38) are as follows: 1. 2107 lb. 2. 8.17 oz. 3. 14,000 lb. 4. 14.25 lb. 5. 133,702,000 lb. 6. 140 lb. **Planet card 2.** Earth weights (to be multiplied by 0.90) are as follows: 1. 0.056 oz. 2. 7561 lb. 3.4,400,000 lb. 4. 715 lb. 5. 27.45 lb. 6. 3 lb. **Planet card 3.** Earth weights (to be multiplied by 0.38) are as follows: 1. 4411.41 lb. 2. 255 lb 3. 950 lb. 4. 20,000 lb. 5. 3 lb. 6. 450,000 lb. **Planet card 4.** Earth weights (to be multiplied by

2.87) are as follows: 1. 123 lb. 2. 734.13 lb. 3. 26,800 lb. 4. 0.09 oz. 5. 4.2 oz. 6. 180,000 lb. **Planet card 5.** Earth weights (to be multiplied by 1.32) are as follows: 1. 15,400 lb. 2. 30,115 lb. 3. 27,600 lb. 4. 2 oz. 5. 21 lb. 6. 325 lb. **Planet card 6.** Earth weights (to be multiplied by 0.93) are as follows: 1. 174 lb. (capybara) 2. 25 lb. 3. 100,000 lb. 4. 5-5.5 oz. 5. 14 lb. 6. 6270 lb. **Planet card 7.** Earth weights (to be multiplied by 1.23) are as follows: 1. 81,982 lb. 2. 8.75 lb. 3. 14-16 oz. 4. 605 lb. 5. 375 lb. 6. 2.5 oz.

Research Resources

The Address Book by Michael Levine. New York: Perigee Books, 1984.

Amazing Days by Randy Harelson. New York: Workman Publishing, 1979.

The Book of Firsts by Patrick Robertson. New York: Bramhall House, 1982.

The Book of Jargon by Don Miller. New York; Macmillan Publishing Co., 1981.

The Book of Lists by David Wallechinsky, Irving Wallace, and Amy Wallace. New York: William Morrow and Co., 1977.

The Book of Lists #2 by Irving Wallace, David Wallechinsky, Amy Wallace, and Sylvia Wallace. New York: William Morrow and Co., 1980.

The Book of Lists #3 by Amy Wallace, David Wallechinsky, and Irving Wallace. New York: William Morrow and Co., 1983.

Chase's Annual Events by William and Helen Chase. Chicago: Contemporary Books, Inc., 1987. (Revised yearly.)

Comparisons by the Diagram Group. New York: St. Martin's Press, 1980.

The Complete Unabridged Super Trivia Encyclopedia by Fred L. Worth. Los Angeles: Brooke House, 1979.

The Contest Book by Ken Dollar, Ruth Reichl, and Susan Subtle. New York: Harmony Books, 1979.

The Dictionary of Misinformation by Tom Burnham. New York: Crowell, 1975.

Dictionary of Occupational Titles, Fourth Edition. U.S. Department of Labor. Washington, DC: 1977.

Dictionary of Word and Phrase Origins by William and Mary Morris. New York: Harper & Row, 1971.

Durations: The Encyclopedia of How Long Things Take by Stuart A. Sandow. New York: New York Times Books, 1977.

Encyclopedia Brown's Record Book of Weird and Wonderful Facts by Donald J. Sobol. New York: Delacorte Press, 1979.

An Exaltation of Larks by James Lipton. New York: Viking Press, 1977.

The Facts on File Visual Dictionary by Jean-Claude Corbeil. New York: Facts on File Publications, 1986.

Famous First Facts by Joseph Nathan Jane. New York: The H.W. Wilson Company, 1981.

Far-Out Facts. Washington, DC: National Geographic Society, 1980.

Fascinating Facts by David Louis. New York: Ridge Press/Crown Publishers, 1977.

The First of Everything by Dennis Sanders. New York: Dell Publishing Co., 1981.

Guinness Book of World Records by Norris McWhirter. New York: Bantam Books, 1986. (Revised yearly.)

Horsefeathers and Other Curious Words by Charles Earle Funk and Charles Earle Funk, Jr. New York: Harper & Row, 1986.

I Hear America Talking by Stuart Berg Flexner. New York: Simon & Schuster, 1976.

Listening to America by Stuart Berg Flexner. New York: Simon & Schuster, 1982.

The National Directory of Addresses and Telephone Numbers edited by Frederick Siles. New York: Concord Reference Books, Inc., 1985.

101 Words and How They Began by Arthur Steckler. New York: Doubleday, 1979.

The People's Almanac by David Wallechinsky and Irving Wallace. Garden City, NY: Doubleday and Co., 1975.

The People's Almanac #2 by David Wallechinsky and Irving Wallace. New York: Bantam Books, 1978.

The People's Almanac #3 by David Wallechinsky and Irving Wallace. New York: William Morrow and Co., 1981.

Simon and Schuster Book of Facts and Fallacies by Rhoda Blumberg. New York: Simon & Schuster, 1983.

The Teacher's Book of Lists by Sheila Madsen and Bette Gould. Santa Monica, CA: Goodyear Publishing, Inc., 1979.

Webster's Biographical Dictionary. Springfield, MA: G. & C. Merriam Company, 1976.

What's Behind the Word by Harold Longman. New York: Coward, McCann, and Geoghegan, 1968.

What's What by David Fisher and Reginald Bragonier, Jr. Maplewood, NJ: Hammond Inc., 1981.

Word Origins and Their Romantic Stories by Wilfred Funk. New York: Bell Publishing Company, 1950.

Words by Paul Dickson. New York: Delacorte Press, 1982.

Words by Jane Sarnoff and Reynold Ruffins. New York: Charles Scribner's Sons, 1981.

The World Almanac Book of Who edited by Hana Umlauf Lane. New York: World Almanac Publications, 1980.

The World Almanac and Book of Facts edited by Hana Umlauf Lane. New York: World Almanac Publications, 1986. (Revised yearly.)

You're Dumber in the Summer by Jim Aylward. New York: Holt, Rinehart & Winston, 1980.

FACT-FINDERS Research Project

NUMBER

NAME OF RESEARCHER

TITLE OF PROJECT

DATE OF COMPLETION

RESEARCH FINDINGS

Keeping Track of Your Sources

Books

Author's last name, first name, Title of Book, City of publication, State: Publishing Company, date of publication, page numbers where information was found.

For example:

> Parker, Tom, In One Day, Boston, Mass.: Houghton Mifflin Company, 1984, page 64.

Encyclopedia

Name of Encyclopedia, Place of publication: Publishing Company, date of publication, volume, page numbers where information was found.

For example:

> Compton's Encyclopedia, Chicago: F. E. Compton Co., 1971, Volume 4 (C/China), pages 56-57.

Magazines/Newspapers

Author's last name, first name, "Title of Article," Title of Magazine/ Newspaper, Volume number (date of publication), page numbers where information was found.

For example:

> Lewis, Mary C., "Magic: West African Roots," Ebony, Vol. 9 No. 4 (October 1981), pages 7-8.

Pamphlet

Title of Pamphlet, Place of publication: Name of organization, date of publication, page numbers where information was found.

For example:

> "Short Course in the Graphic Arts," Dayton, Ohio: Mead Papers,1973, page 14.

(NOTE: All of this information is not always available for pamphlets. If that is the case, simply give as much information as you can find.)

Fact-Finders Certificate of Merit

This is to certify that

____

has successfully met the challenge of the Fact-Finders research investigations.

____
Date

____
Research Supervisor